POSTCARD GRAPHICS

The Best Advertising and Promotion Design

First published in the United States of America by:

Rockport Publishers, Inc.
146 Granite Street
Rockport, Massachusetts 01966-1299
Telephone: (508) 546-9590
Fax: (508) 546-7141

Distributed to the book trade and art trade in the United States by:

North Light, an imprint of
F & W Publications
1507 Dana Avenue
Cincinnati, Ohio 45207
Telephone: (800) 289-0963

Other Distribution by:

Rockport Publishers, Inc.
Rockport, Massachusetts 01966-1299

ISBN 1-56496-334-9

10 9 8 7 6 5 4 3 2 1

Designer: Minnie Cho

Manufactured in China by Regent Publishing Services Limited

Cover credits: (See diagram below)

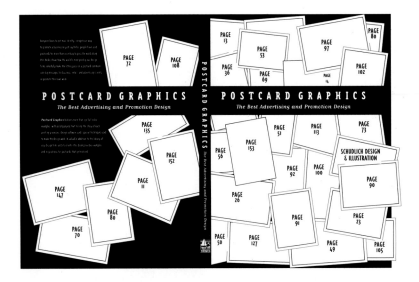

POSTCARD GRAPHICS

The Best Advertising and Promotion Design

Rockport Publishers
Rockport, Massachusetts

Distributed by North Light Books, Cincinnati, Ohio

INTRODUCTION

by Stefan Sagmeister

I love postcards because of their many confinements. First, there is the size: they can be no larger than 5 1/2" x 8 1/2", no smaller than 3 1/2" x 5" or the post office will hit you with a surcharge. Second, there is the weight: if you're over one ounce, the postage goes up. Clients love to stay under. And thickness: you'd better be between 1/7000 and 1/2 of an inch if you want your postcard to be classified as standard mail. There's a designated area for the address, another one for the stamp.

A lot of confining rules always leads to rule-defying questions: Can we design a card that mails flat but becomes three-dimensional when received? A poster that folds down to standard postcard size? Can we attach little objects? Can we die-cut?

In general, postcards are democratic: They can be produced by anybody, for almost no money at all. They can be rubber-stamped on chipboard, photocopied or laser-printed on card stock. The whole run can be hand-painted. There are e-mail postcards that don't require printing at all.

Slicker but still inexpensive looks can be achieved utilizing computerized, short-run color printing technology. On the high end almost every printing and production technique can be utilized to make them; there are die-cut, hot-stamped, fold-out, pop-up, v-hold, concertina, panorama, wooden, plastic, holographic, and collapsible cards out there. I have seen cards with glass stones and other cheap jewelry applied to them, cards with Alka-Seltzer packages glued onto them and cards with condoms attached. One line of cards features plants growing out of its paper, and another comprises cards that, dissolved in water, yield a whole family of living animals.

A French journalist received a bullet in the mail with a postcard stating "This one's for you." A subsequent police investigation proved it to be a professional gag for a new James Bond movie. He sued.

I have a box in my bedroom where I keep great mailings received over the years. Even though I get around a dozen pieces of printed material every day, the box is still rather empty. An avalanche of junk mail is not only polluting the countryside with waste dumps (and ridding us of some trees on the side), but it also plays a major part in the visual pollution of our lives. Our eyes feel contaminated after we leaf through heaps of printed mail where each piece tries to shout its offer louder than the others. All of them are mute, as they cancel each other out.

The task of the designer is not only to break through that clutter, but also to enhance our lives with something intriguing and unique. My favorite piece of junk mail is a fully addressed, stamped, evil-smelling sock sent to me, without envelope, by a friend. The U.S. Postal Service actually delivered it to me.

There are a number of cards in this book that I would love to have in my aforementioned box. These pieces go beyond the task of delivering a message or solving a client's problem. The love, care, and even the anxiety that went into them during the design process rubs off on the recipient and gives a minuscule bit of delight to the viewer.

When creating postcards there are two choices: I can either give birth to junk and be part of the visual pollution machinery, or I become the creator of that tiny spark of joy and present an itsy bitsy piece of pleasure to a person. Do I want to be a polluter or a creator? Polluter or creator? Tough one.

Stefan Sagmeister
runs Sagmeister Inc.
in New York City,
a company specializing
in graphic design for the
music industries.

ROSENWORLD

BEAUTY IS IN THE MIND OF THE BEHELD

PRODUCTION

INTERACTIVE ENTERTAINMENT   GAMING CD MAG

new lower prices!

YES! Send my subscription to IE-the CD ROM Game Magazine.

	Retail	USA	Canada & Europe	Others
1 year-12 issues	$119	$59 (save $60!)	$79	$99

Name (please print)

Phone   Address   State   Zip

City   Expiration Date

Bill me   Credit Card #

Date   Signature

Payment must be in US Funds. Vermont residents add 5% tax. Allow 6 weeks for processing. Visa and Mastercard accepted. FAX. 810.562.3624 Phone: 800.562.3624

SOURCE 97512

send your friend a note

interactive entertainment

EVENT
ANNOUNCEMENTS

HOLIDAY

50% Balance Kreuzmiren C 50% 50% M 50% 50% 25

The firm based this series on the concept of printer make-ready sheets for materials produced by the Production Club of Greater Washington, a professional group. Inspired by the collaged, layered, multiple, often accidental patterns that one sees in make-ready sheets, the club used QuarkXPress and traditional overlays to create the effects.

FROM THE BIG IDEA TO THE SMALLEST DETAIL

Join us to discuss Grafik Communications' promotion for ESSE ™ by Gilbert, a new recycled paper. Panelists Judy Kirpich and Melanie Bass of Grafik Communications, Roger Chavez of Virginia Lithograph, copywriter Jake Pollard, Katie Gekker of Huffman Press, and Su McLaughlin of Gilbert Paper will describe the creative and manufacturing challenges they encountered while developing this exciting, multi-faceted piece.

Embassy Suites Hotel Wisconsin at Western

THE SCENES: AND THE PRINTED PIECE

...rtunity for a look at three different photo set-ups in an actual

1

Join Barry Soorenko and his staff photographers in

...ns and discussions covering all issues affecting your photo shoot.

...HINGTON, INC.

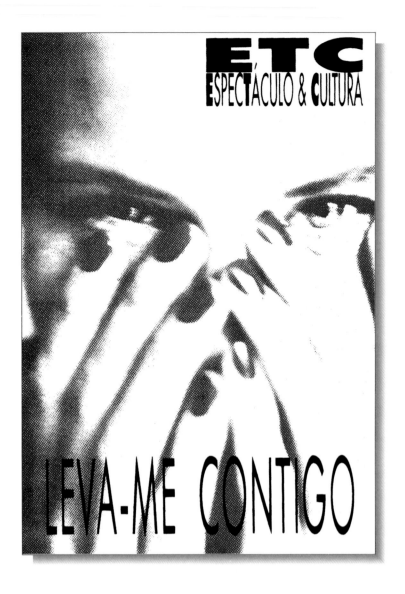

ETC
ESPECTÁCULO & CULTURA

LEVA-ME CONTIGO

Design Firm
Mário Aurélio & Associates

Art Director
Mário Aurélio

Designers
Mário Aurélio, Rosa Maia

Original Size
6" x 4" (15 cm x 10 cm)

Client
Cinema Novo, CRL

Printing
2-color offset

Produced in Macromedia FreeHand, this was a promotional mailing touting a newspaper of culture and show business.

Design Firm
Franek Design Associates Inc.

Art Director
David Franek

Designer
Max McNeil

Illustrators
Max McNeil, David Franek

Original Size
3 1/2" x 5" (9 cm x 13 cm);
4" x 6" (10 cm x 15 cm)

Client
Production Club of Greater Washington

Purpose/Occasion
Calendar of events

Printing
Three PMS colors on two sides

Design Firm
Mário Aurélio & Associates

Art Director
Mário Aurélio

Designers
Mário Aurélio, Rosa Maia

Original Size
4" x 6" (10 cm x 15 cm)

Client
Terminal X

Purpose/Occasion
Special Fryday

Printing
4-color offset

The postcards, made in Macromedia
FreeHand and Adobe Photoshop,
stayed very interesting and brought
many people to the disco.

Design Firm
Sayles Graphic Design

**Art Director/
Designer**
John Sayles

Original Size
Various

Client
Hotel Fort Des Moines

Printing
Offset

Developed to invite guests to a gala 75th anniversary celebration, this 3-D cigar box actually includes vintage postcard reproductions inside the box, along with other memorabilia.

Art Director
Ann Samul

Illustrator
Gabardine Slax

Original Size
4" x 6" (10 cm x 15 cm)

Client
11 Pacific Street Art Gallery

Printing
Photocopy, letterpress

The 11 Pacific Street Art Gallery likes to do mailings at least once a month, but it's important to keep costs down. Because the gallery has free access to a photocopier, all of its postcards are black-and-white. The pen-and-ink drawing created for the postcard complements the words on the reverse, printed on an antique letterpress the organization has on premises.

Design Firm
Leo Pharmaceuticals

Art Director/Designer
Vibeke Nødskov

Original Size
3" x 8 1/2" (8 cm x 22 cm)

Client
Leo Pharmaceuticals

Printing
3-color silk screen

This postcard/paper bag is an invitation for doctors to join an event/exhibition. It says to bring the invitation along, and then the bag gets filled with "glogg-mix" (spices and herbs for a hot wine drink). A little handle, rolled in a neon sticker, is actually the recipe for the drink.

Design Firm
Athanasius Design

Art Director/Designer
Jeffrey Wallace

Photographer
A. Blair

Original Size
4" x 6" (10 cm x 15 cm)

Client
TRIO Salon

Purpose/Occasion
3rd anniversary party

Printing
2-color (metallic) and varnish

TRIO is a new but very successful beauty salon with a strong commitment to corporate identity exposure. The card serves as an invitation to an anniversary reception at a popular musical venue, and as a promotion piece. It includes an Elite agency model with a (mock) tattoo with the company logo on his arm, a customized anniversary cake, and champagne flutes.

Three's the Charm

THE TRIO CELEBRATE THEIR THIRD ANNIVERSARY

Design Firm
Lev Laboratorio di Comunicazione

Art Director/Designer
Angelo Ferara

Original Size
8 1/2" x 4" (22 cm x 10 cm)

Client
Lev Laboratorio de Comunicazione

Printing
2-color, die-cut

This postcard announces the communication agency's name-change to LEV, short for Levis Elephantis Visibilitas—"the visibility of the light elephant" in Latin. This phrase becomes represented on paper, where "light" is a white piece of paper; "elephant" can upturn its trunk; "visibility" because the postcard becomes a little sculpture.

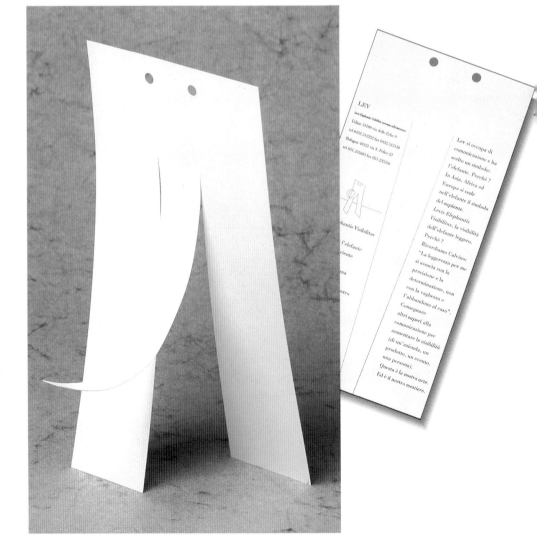

Design Firm
Duo Design

Designer
Jose Rui Fernando

Illustrator
Peter Kuper

Original Size
6" x 4" (15 cm x 10 cm)

Client
Internacional de Banda Desenhada do Porto

Printing
4-color offset

Created for a comic-strip exhibition in Portugal that featured Kuper's work, the art was created from a cut stencil sprayed with enamel paint, with watercolor and colored pencil added. Type was added later with a computer.

Design Firm
Lamont-Doherty Earth Observatory

Designer
Janice Aitchison

Photographer
Michael Gaffney

Original Size
5" x 7" (13 cm x 18 cm)

Purpose/Occasion
1995 American Geophysical Union meeting

Printing
Indigo press

Announcing a reception for an annual meeting of Earth scientists, this card features layout in QuarkXPress and a photo manipulated in Adobe Photoshop using Adobe Gallery Effects.

Design Firm
Lamont-Doherty Earth Observatory

Designer
Janice Aitchison

Illustrator
José Ortega

Original Size
5" x 7" (13 cm x 18 cm)

Client
Lamont-Doherty Earth Observatory

Purpose/Occasion
1994 American Geophysical Union meeting

Printing
Indigo press

Announcing a reception for an annual meeting of earth scientists, this card features layout in QuarkXPress with artwork stretched a bit to fit the layout. LDEO commissioned the original artwork for its newsletter; using the cover design in several different pieces tied together announcements of other Lamont events.

IF YOU PLAN TO ATTEND AGU IN SAN FRANCISCO NEXT MONTH, PLEASE JOIN US FOR A LAMONT RECEPTION 5:30 P.M.–7:00 P.M. MONDAY DECEMBER 5, 1994 THE SUTTER III ROOM HOLIDAY INN UNION SQUARE 480 SUTTER STREET

Design Firm
The Design Company

Art Director/Designer
Busha Husak

Printing
Laser and by hand

These postcards were invitations to a "Wok Luck" dinner in which the artist applied the concept of a "potluck" dinner and added an Asian and Indian flair. The base of the invitation is cut-up corrugated Chinese and Japanese food cartons. Created in QuarkXPress, the labels were printed with coffee-soaked sponges. The postage stamps are commemorative of the 1996 Chinese New Year—keeping within the theme of the event.

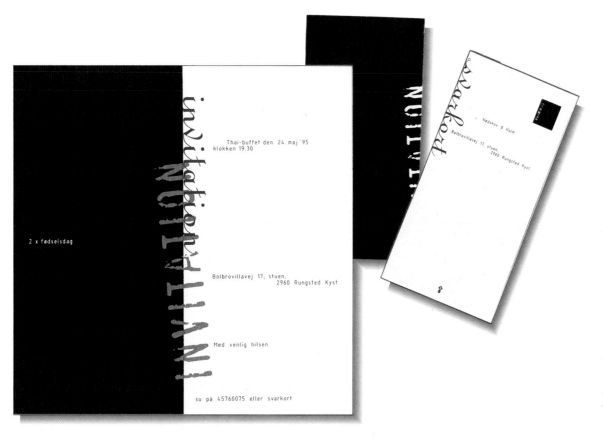

Art Director/Designer
Vibeke Nødskov

Original Size
8 1/2" x 8 1/2" (22 cm x 22 cm)

Printing
3- and 2-color offset

This card is a double birthday invitation for a married couple. Black-and-white symbolizes male/female yin and yang. Moreover, the choice of colors and typefaces for the word "invitation" emphasizes the duality. The recipient cuts the card in half as indicated, places a stamp where indicated, writes the response, and mails the response part.

Design Firm
Misha Design Studio

Designer
Dina Barsky

Illustrator
Michael Lenn

Original Size
6" x 4" (15 cm x 10 cm)

Client
Lasell Institute for Fashion Technology

Printing
Process offset

This invitation for a fashion show began with a freehand drawing of a female in a theatrical evening gown. The image depicts the motion and extravagance characteristic of a fashion show. The dress and hair are free-flowing and free-form.

Design Firm
Fresno Pacific College

Art Director/
Designer/
Photographer
John Lopes

Original Size
5 1/2" x 5 1/2" (14 cm x 14 cm)

Client
Alumni Relations

Purpose/Occasion
Phonathon Announcement

Printing
2-color lithography

Composed in Adobe PageMaker, this postcard incorporates wrapped/fitted text with a photograph of a phone receiver. The designer scanned the receiver directly on the scanner bed.

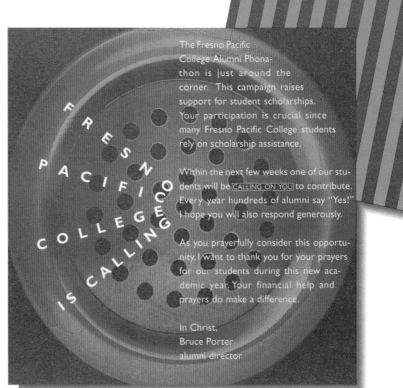

1717 S. Chestnut Ave.
Fresno, CA 93702

Non Profit Org.
U.S. Postage
PAID
Permit No. 2561
Fresno, CA

FRESNO PACIFIC COLLEGE IS CALLING

The Fresno Pacific College Alumni Phonathon is just around the corner. This campaign raises support for student scholarships. Your participation is crucial since many Fresno Pacific College students rely on scholarship assistance.

Within the next few weeks one of our students will be CALLING ON YOU to contribute. Every year hundreds of alumni say "Yes!" I hope you will also respond generously.

As you prayerfully consider this opportunity, I want to thank you for your prayers for our students during this new academic year. Your financial help and prayers do make a difference.

In Christ,
Bruce Porter
alumni director

Design Firm
Cook and Shanosky Assoc. Inc.

Art Director/Designer
Roger Cook

Original Size
4" x 6" (10 cm x 15 cm)

Client
March of Dimes

Printing
2-color

This card, punched eighteen times for eighteen holes, is a reminder to attend a benefit golf outing. The designer produced it in QuarkXPress.

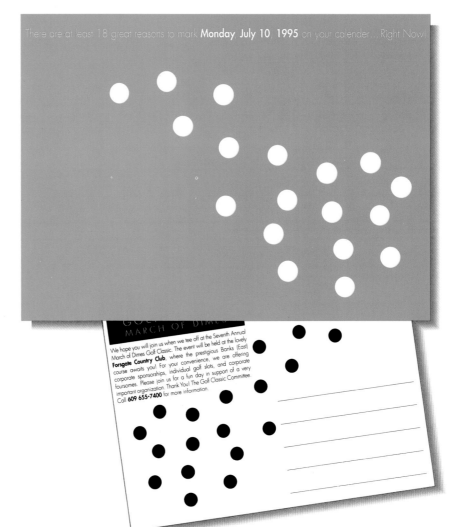

There are at least 18 great reasons to mark **Monday, July 10, 1995** on your calender... Right Now!

GOLF MARCH OF DIMES

We hope you will join us when we tee off at the Seventh Annual March of Dimes Golf Classic. The event will be held at the lovely **Forsgate Country Club**, where the prestigious Banks (East) course awaits you! For your convenience, we are offering corporate sponsorships, individual golf slots, and corporate foursomes. Please join us for a fun day in support of a very important organization. Thank You! The Golf Classic Committee. Call **609 655·7400** for more information.

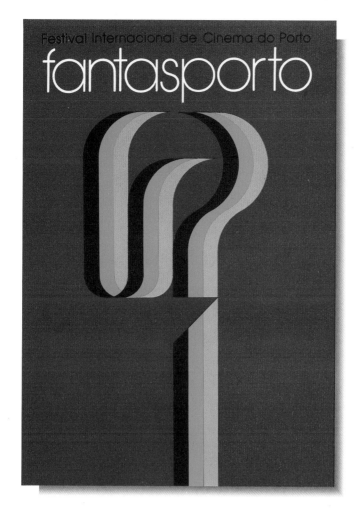

Design Firm
Mário Aurélio & Associates

Art Director
Mário Aurélio

Designers
Mário Aurélio, Rosa Maia

Original Size
6" x 4" (15 cm x 10 cm)

Client
Fantasporto/Film Festival

Purpose/Occasion
International Movie Festival

Printing
4-color offset

The client likes this card, made in Macromedia FreeHand, because of the bright colors and lettering.

Design Firm
Beckman Instruments Inc.

Art Director/Designer
Teri Beauchamp

Original Size
6" x 4" (15 cm x 10 cm)

Client
Beckman Instruments Inc.

Printing
Lithography

Every year the company holds a special event for long service employees— employees that have been with the company for 5 years or more. The company gave the event a Caribbean theme— "Carnivalé: An Anniversary in Paradise." Having held the party at the same location for more than 20 years, the company changed venues this year; the design staff created this postcard in Adobe Illustrator and Photoshop to remind attendees.

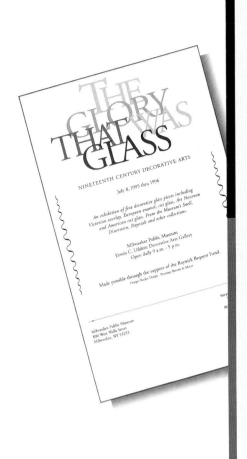

Design Firm
Becker Design

Art Director
Neil Becker

Designers
Neil Becker, Drew M. Dallet

Photographer
Joanne K. Peterson

Original Size
11" x 6 1/2" (28 cm x 16 cm)

Client
Milwaukee Public Museum

Purpose/Occasion
"The Glory that Was Glass" Exhibit

Printing
4-color lithography

Used as a promotional piece for the Milwaukee Public Museum's 19th-century glass exhibit, this design also appears as a 24" x 36" (61 cm x 91 cm) poster. The postcard was created in Adobe Photoshop and QuarkXPress.

Design Firm
Sagmeister Inc.

Art Director/ Designer/ Client
Stefan Sagmeister

Photographers
Karolina, Karl, Christine, Andrea, and Veronica Sagmeister

Original Size
4" x 6" (10 cm x 15 cm)

Printing
Offset

This is an invitation for a 30th birthday party, so it was logical to show an overview of the last 30 years.

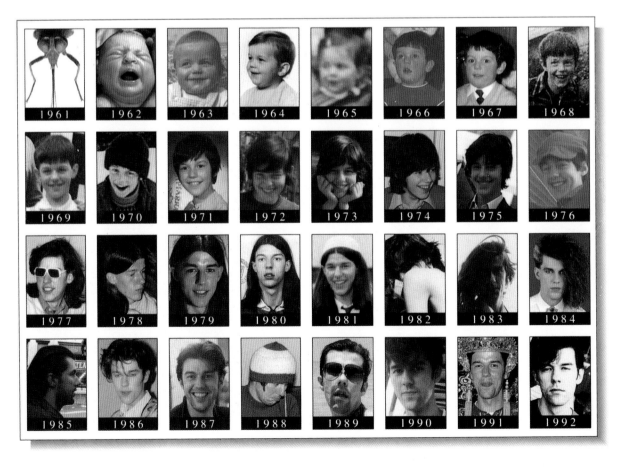

Design Firm
Stoltze Design/Visual Dialogue

Designers
Fritz Klaetke, Eric Norman, Clifford Stoltze

Original Size
4" x 6" (10 cm x 15 cm)

Client
AIGA Boston

Printing
4-color, silk screen

The designer conceived an announcement
for a special double-header lecture as a way
to promote husband and wife (P. Scott Makela
and Laurie Haysock Makela). The designer came
up with the title "For Better or For Worse."

Design Firm
Mars

Art Director
Susan Sanderson

Designer
Michelle Vredvoogd

Original Size
8 1/2" x 5 1/2" (22 cm x 14 cm)

Client
EQ

Printing
4-color process, one offset

Laid out in QuarkXPress, this
card invites vendors to visit
a booth at a convention.

The Natives are friendly.

Start getting your sales tribe ready for new Dashboard 95 and Sidekick 95, from Starfish Software. Dashboard 95 is the Windows 95 version of the award-winning Windows utility, and Sidekick 95 is the Windows 95 version of the #1 best-selling personal organizer. Both apps are 100% Windows 95 native applications and are shipping NOW. They're not just compatible, they speak fluent 32-bit! Your customers will go wild. Don't miss out! Order now from your distributor!

Tech Data
1-800-237-8931

INGRAM MICRO
1-800-456-8000

Starfish Soft
1700 Scotts

Go Native!

Starfish Software Announces Dashboard® 95 and Sidekick® 95, native 32-bit applications for Windows® 95. Coming soon to your village.

Design Firm
Free-Range Chicken Ranch

Art Director/Designer
Kelli Christman

Illustrator
Donna Gilbert

Original Size
4" x 6" (10 cm x 15 cm)

Client
Starfish Software

Printing
Offset

A series, the client wanted fun, inexpensive cards to send out announcing their new versions of software programs. Cost and timing were critical to concept—this was a rush project done in QuarkXPress.

Watch How Fast These Starfish Run

Windows 95 is the next wave in PC performance. And new Dashboard 95 and Sidekick 95 are here to help your customers manage their ocean of information. Dashboard 95 is the Windows 95 version of our award-winning Windows 95 utility, and Sidekick 95 is the Windows 95 version of the #1 best-selling personal organizer. Both apps are 100% Windows 95 native applications and are available now. They're not just compatible, they operate on 32-bit bytes! These robust, speedy Starfish Software apps are sure to make a huge splash. Don't miss out! Order now from your distributor!

Starfish Software, In
1700 Green Hills Rd
Scotts Valley, CA 9

Tech Data
1-800-237-8931

INGRAM MICRO
1-800-456-8000

This Starfish takes 32-bit bytes.

Sidekick® 95 and Dashboard® 95 are specially designed for Windows® 95. Available now coast to coast.

YOU'RE INVITED!

Design Firm
Art Chantry

Art Director/Designer
Art Chantry

Original Size
4 1/2" x 8" (11 cm x 20 cm)

Client
Larry's Market

Printing
Offset

This invitation promotes the grand opening of a gourmet/deli-style supermarket.

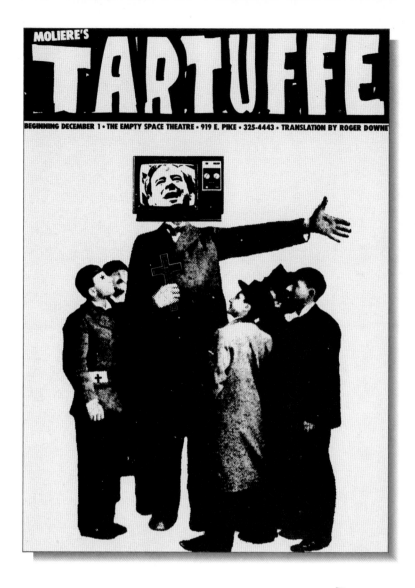

MOLIERE'S TARTUFFE

BEGINNING DECEMBER 1 • THE EMPTY SPACE THEATRE • 919 E. PIKE • 325-4443 • TRANSLATION BY ROGER DOWNE

Design Firm
Art Chantry

**Art Director/
Designer/
Illustrator**
Art Chantry

Original Size
8 1/2" x 4" (22 cm x 10 cm)

Client
Empty Space Theatre

Printing
Offset

This promotes a production of Molière's 17th-century play *Tartuffe*—a 20th century update of the farcical tale of religious hypocrisy—with Tartuffe as a television evangelist.

Design Firm
Kan Tai-keung Design & Associates Ltd.

Art Director
Freeman Lau Siu Hong

Designer
Pamela Low Pui Hang

Original Size
5" x 7" (13 cm x 18 cm)

Client
Hong Kong Designers Association

Title
"A Tale of Two Squares"

The design of two squares with the exhibitors' names on it was an idea from the coincidence of the two exhibition places: Times Square and Exchange Square.

Design Firm
Segura Inc.

Art Director/Designer
Carlos Segura

Photographer
Geof Kern

Original Size
6 1/2" x 10 1/2"
(16 cm x 27 cm)

Client
The Merchandise Mart—Neocon

Printing
4-color

The Neocon cards promote
a yearly conference on
interior design.

15TH ANNIVERSARY
CHILDHAVEN POLO

Design Firm
Bartels & Company

Art Director
David Bartels

Designer
John Postlewaite

Illustrator
Gary Kelley

Original Size
9" x 6" (23 cm x 15 cm)

Client
Childhaven

Purpose/Occasion
Charity Event Reminder

Printing
4-color lithography

The illustrator—who works exclusively in pastels—rendered the illustration for this 15th anniversary of a St. Louis-based charity fund-raiser. The charity used the postcard as a reminder of the upcoming event.

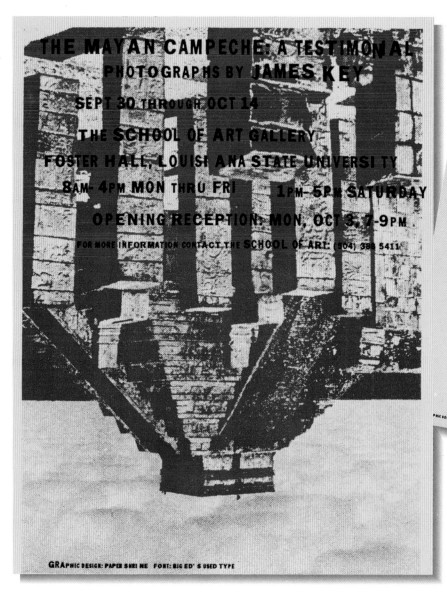

THE MAYAN CAMPECHE: A TESTIMONIAL
PHOTOGRAPHS BY JAMES KEY
SEPT 30 THROUGH OCT 14
THE SCHOOL OF ART GALLERY
FOSTER HALL, LOUISIANA STATE UNIVERSITY
8AM- 4PM MON THRU FRI   1PM- 5PM SATURDAY
OPENING RECEPTION: MON, OCT 3, 7-9PM
FOR MORE INFORMATION CONTACT THE SCHOOL OF ART: (504) 388 5411

GRAPHIC DESIGN: PAPER SHRINE   FONT: BIG ED'S USED TYPE

Design Firm
Paper Shrine

Art Director/Designer
Paul Dean

Original Size
5 1/2" x 4" (14 cm x 10 cm)

Client
Louisiana State University

Purpose/Occasion
Art Exhibition

Printing
Photocopy

The subject of this photo exhibition—
the Mayan Campeche—reminded the
designer of a typeface designed by
Edwin Utermohlen of Big Ed's Used Type.
The designer put the two together,
and photocopied the cards to stay
under budget.

Design Firm
Howard Levy Design

Art Director/
Designer/
Illustrator
Howard Levy

Original Size
7" x 7" (18 cm x 18 cm)

Client
Jewish Community Center of
Greater Monmouth, New Jersey

Printing
Offset

This postcard is the first in a series of
mailings publicizing a fund-raising auction
with a safari theme. Each mailing will have
a different animal, with a different animal
pattern in a different color.

Design Firm
Mervil Paylor Design

Art Director/Designer
Mervil M. Paylor

Original Size
9" x 6" (23 cm x 15 cm)

Client
Paper Skyscraper

Printing
1-color offset

Paper Skyscraper—a little store offering books, stationery, home furnishings, kitchen accessories, toys, and bath products—has an annual "Hog Wild Sale," which makes rich fodder for humorous copy and imagery each year. The 1996 theme was the Greek myth of Pygmalion.

Design Firm
Area-Strategic Design

Art Director
Antonio Romano

Designer
Stefania Anroini

Original Size
8 1/2" x 4 1/2" (22 cm x 11 cm)

Client
Finmeccanica

Purpose/Occasion
Asian Eurospace '96 convention

Printing
Lithography

This postcard strives to relate the tradition of the past to the newest technological evolution.

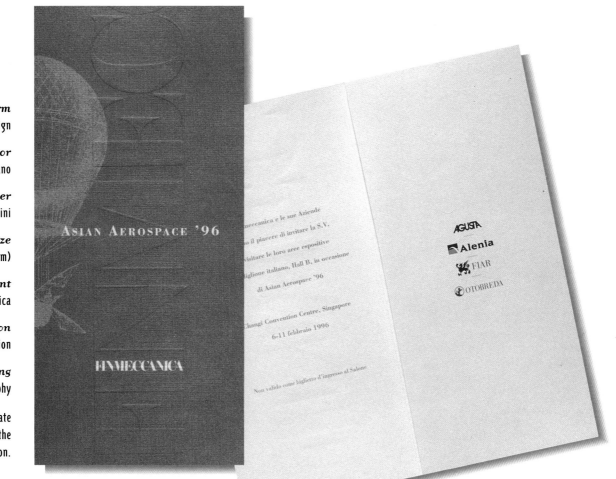

Design Firm
Thompson/Kerr

Art Director
Scott Lee

Designer
Andrea Freedlund

Photographer
Picture Perfect

Original Size
6" x 8" (15 cm x 20 cm)

Client
Sprint

Printing
CMYK and metallic gold

The firm designed this postcard as an initial teaser for the Sprint Business Users' conference taking place in May 1996. A series of three brochures followed with additional information. The designer created the piece in QuarkXPress and Adobe Illustrator.

Design Firm
Bartels & Company

Art Director
David Bartels

Designer
Brian Barclay

Illustrator
Braldt Bralds

Original Size
4" x 6" (10 cm x 15 cm)

Client
St. Louis Zoo

Place
Stamp
Here

ZOO
FARI
1989

St. Louis Zoo Friends Association
St. Louis Zoo—Forest Park
St. Louis, MO
63110

St. Louis Zoo Friends Association
invites you to attend a

ZOOFARI 1989 PRE-PARTY
"Conservation Celebration"

Friday, June Sixteenth
Six-Thirty until Eight O'Clock
The Living World Rotunda

This portion of your invitation
entitles you to VIP Parking on the North Lot St. Louis Zoo,
and will admit you to the Preparty

☐ Yes, I will attend the Pre-party
Number attending _____
☐ No, I will be unable to attend.
Mr./Mrs. _____

Please respond by June 5, 1989

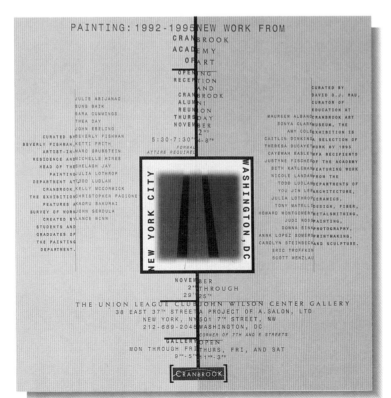

Design Firm
Carole Goodman

**Art Director/
Designer/
Photographer**
Carole Goodman

Original Size
8 1/2" x 8 1/2" (22 cm x 22 cm)

Client
Cranbrook Academy of Art

Printing
Offset lithography

This piece promotes simultaneous openings of two Cranbrook Academy of Art galleries in different cities. Recipients choose which opening to attend; a perforation separates the two invitations. When the recipient tears the invitation, the information that is common to both exhibits, running over the perforation, wraps around the card.

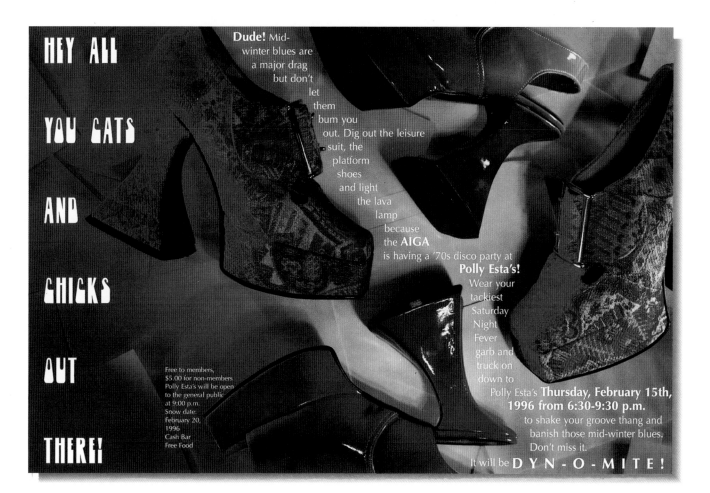

Dude! Midwinter blues are a major drag but don't let them bum you out. Dig out the leisure suit, the platform shoes and light the lava lamp because the **AIGA** is having a '70s disco party at **Polly Esta's!** Wear your tackiest Saturday Night Fever garb and truck on down to Polly Esta's **Thursday, February 15th, 1996 from 6:30-9:30 p.m.** to shake your groove thang and banish those mid-winter blues. Don't miss it. It will be **DYN-O-MITE!**

HEY ALL YOU CATS AND CHICKS OUT THERE!

Free to members, $5.00 for non-members Polly Esta's will be open to the general public at 9:00 p.m. Snow date: February 20, 1996 Cash Bar Free Food

Design Firm
Heather Yale Creative

Designer
Heather Yale

Photographer
Michael Kressley

Original Size
6" x 9" (15 cm x 23 cm)

Printing
Indigo press

The designer created this postcard with the fascination and character of the 1970s in mind. AIGA/Boston sent it to members as an invitation to a '70s party, encouraging them to truck on down and check it out.

Designer
Arlo Bigazzi

Original Size
6" x 4" (15 cm x 10 cm)

Client
Materiali Sonori

Purpose/Occasion
CD release

Printing
Lithography

MATERIALI SONORI

VIA TRIESTE 35 . 52027 . SAN GIOVANNI VALDARNO . PH. 055/943868 . FAX 055/9120370 . DISTRIBUITI IN ITALIA DA C.G.D. SpA - A TIME WARNER COMPANY

wim
MERTENS
jérémiades
cd . 1295700812

Art Director/
Designer/
Photographer
Gary Krueger

Original Size
3 1/2" x 5 1/2" (9 cm x 14 cm)

Printing
Process offset

Design Firm
Schudlich Design & Illustration

Art Director/
Designer/
Illustrator
Steve Schudlich

Original Size
6" x 4" (15 cm x 10 cm)

Client
Ceci Bartels Associates

Purpose/Occasion
Holiday promotion

The firm wanted a clever, inexpensive greeting card to send to its clients, sending this "Great Art Is Always In Season" card at Christmas, Valentine's Day, and Halloween.

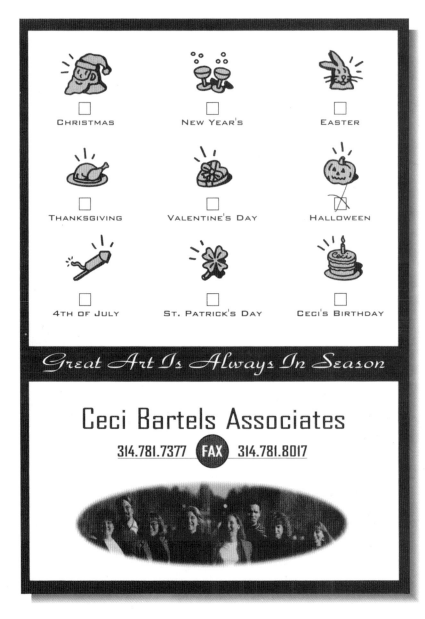

© 1995, Jacqueline Comstock (914) 987-8314

**Designer/
Illustrator**
Jacqueline Comstock

Original Size
5" x 7" (13 cm x 18 cm)

Purpose/Occasion
Self-promotion

Printing
4-color, ganged up

The holiday season is a perfect opportunity to create a self-promotion piece. For this illustration, digitally manipulated stock photography (the angel statue, clouds, and wing feathers) combines with a hand-painted Earth.

Design Firm
Schudlich Design & Illustration

**Art Director/
Designer/
Illustrator**
Steve Schudlich

Original Size
4" x 6" (10 cm x 15 cm)

Client
Ceci Bartels Associates

Purpose/Occasion
Christmas

In an effort to create a greeting card that was interactive, the designer came up with the concept of a holiday ornament cut-out. Printing small postcards allowed the firm to send the cards liberally to its large client base.

The Ceci Bartels Associates
Official
Self Promotional Holiday Ornament

- Photography
- Illustration
- Computer Illustration
- High-end Digital Assembly
- Graphic Design

St Louis 314.781.7377
24 hour fax 314.781.8017
Chicago 312.786.1560
New York 212.912.1877

happy holidays

Hey, you're a creative type, stick a paper clip or something through the hole.

cut along this line

Design © Illustration / Stephen Schudlich

Ceci Bartels Assoc.
AGENTS FOR ARTISTS
3286 Ivanhoe/St. Louis, MO 63139

Thanks for the work!

Design Firm
Cosaro and Associates

**Art Director/
Designer/
Illustrator**
Rick A. Cosaro

Original Size
8 1/2" x 5 1/2" (22 cm x 14 cm)

Printing
Indigo press

This postcard was a self-promotion
Christmas card, representing the
magic of the season. The card was
produced using Adobe Illustrator
and Adobe Photoshop.

December 25

mary christmas and have a nifty ninety three

midget
DESIGN

...tmas greetings from the little nipper.
...onmouth Avenue Vancouver, BC Canada V5R 5R9 (604) 435-4965

Design Firm
Midget Design

Art Director/
Designer/
Client
Nancy Yeasting

Original Size
9" x 4" (23 cm x 10 cm)

Purpose/Occasion
Christmas

Printing
2-color lithography

A goofy, "untraditional" postcard. Pictures were scanned from vintage TV novelty books and cleaned up/distorted on HEW system. To save expenses, the printer ganged this postcard with another client's print job, and the design firm traded services with the printer.

Design Firm
David Bamundo Illustration

Designer/Illustrator
David Bamundo

Original Size
6" x 4" (15 cm x 10 cm)

The designer sent out this postcard—created in Adobe Illustrator and Photoshop—to friends, family, and selected clients. Calling his creation, "Rudy's New Doo," the designer lowered the resolution in Photoshop to give it a soft feel.

Design Firm
Lorraine Williams Illustration

**Art Director/
Designer/
Illustrator**
Lorraine Williams

Original Size
6 1/2" x 9" (16 cm x 23 cm)

Printing
4-color process

This mixed media (pastels, water-color, colored pencils) piece was used as a Christmas greeting card to promote the illustrator's work.

Design Firm
The Leonhardt Group

Designer
Dennis Clouse, Traci Daberko

Illustrator
Artists represented by Pat Hackett

Photographer
Photographers represented by Pat Hackett

Original Size
4 1/2" x 5 1/2" (11 cm x 14 cm)

Client
Pat Hackett

Purpose/Occasion
Sales Promotion

Printing
Offset color process (both sides)

Pat Hackett Journeys 1995: This collection of postcards
was designed to illustrate the various talents of the
photographers and illustrators that Pat Hackett
represents. This promotion doubles as a Christmas card;
the postmarks on the back come from a collection of
antique postcards. Each illustrator or photographer
created a representation to match the name of an
American town having to do with Christmas.

Illustrator
James Marsh

Original Size
6 1/2" x 4 1/2" (16 cm x 11 cm)

Client
Population Concern

Purpose/Occasion
Christmas card

The client requested that this painting, titled "New Improved Yuletide," appear on this card for the charity Population Concern.

Design Firm
Mustardseed Enterprises

Designer/ Illustrator/ Photographer
Karen L. Naile

Original Size
6" x 4" (15 cm x 10 cm)

Printing
4-color process

Modern Postcard did the printing. The piece was done as a freehand illustration in colored pencil over watercolor washes with airbrushing. The back side contains a freehand illustration of the logo and typesetting provided by Modern Postcard.

pas·sion \'pash-en\ *n* [ME fr. OF, fr. LL *passion-*, *passio* suffering, being acted upon, fr. L *passus*, pp. of *pati* to suffer — more at PATIENT] (12c) **1** *often cap* **a** : the sufferings of Christ between the night of the Last Supper and his death **b** : an ontario based on a gospel narrative of the Passion **2** *obs* : SUFFERING **3** : the state or capacity of being acted on by external agents or forces **4 a** (1) : EMOTION <his ruling ~ is greed> (2) *pl* : the emotions as distinguished from reason **b** : intense driving or over-mastering feeling or conviction <driven to paint by a ~ beyond her control> **c** : an outbreak of anger **5 a** : ardent affec-tion : LOVE **b** : a strong liking or desire for or devotion to some activity, object or concept **c** : sexual desire **d** : an object of desire or deep interest — **pas·sion·less** \-les\ *adj*

passion

spark

[GK *spearea*; akin too MD *sparke* *spargan* to swell] (bef. 12c)

1 a : a small particle of a burning substance thrown out by a body in combustion or remaining when combustion is nearly completed **b** : a hot glowing particle struck from a larger mass; esp: one heated by friction<produce a ~ by striking flint with steel> **2 a** : a luminous disruptive electrical discharge of very short duration between two conductors separated by a gas (as air) **b** : mechanism controlling the discharge in a soark plug **3** : SPARKLE, FLASH **4** : something that sets off a sudden force <provided the ~ that helped the team to rally> **5** : a latent particle capable of growth or developing : GERM <still retains a ~ of decency> **6** : *pl but sing in constr* :a radio operator on a ship

Design Firm
Stoltze Design

Art Director
Clifford Stoltze

Designers
Clifford Stoltze
Peter Fawell

Original Size
4" x 6" (10 cm x 15 cm)

Purpose/Occasion
Holiday greeting cards

A combination of QuarkXPress and Adobe Photoshop was incorporated in the design of these type-only postcards, which promote the studio.

Design Firm
T.H.S.

Designer
Katharine Tatterson

Illustrator
James Marsh

Original Size
6" x 4" (15 cm x 10 cm)

Client
British Union for the Abolition of Vivisection

Title
"Spot"

Anti-vivisection Christmas card sold in aid of the British Union for the Abolition of Vivisection to raise funds to fight against animal experimentation.

Designer
Eric Kohler

Original Size
6" x 4" (15 cm x 10 cm)

Client
Paul Donzella

Purpose/Occasion
Promotion for gallery

Printing
Offset

The designer made this Valentine mailer in Adobe Illustrator for a gallery that sells 1930s–1950s furniture and decorative objects. The photograph is of a table designed in the 1960s by T. H. Robsjohn Gibbings. The design objective was to create a card with a feeling of the period.

Design Firm
Toni Schowalter Design

Art Director/ Designer/ Illustrator
Toni Schowalter

Original Size
5" x 7" (13 cm x 18 cm)

Client
Mancini Duffy

Printing
Offset, two Pantone colors

Designing in Adobe Illustrator, Mancini Duffy used this card as a holiday greeting for its clients. It was also used to announce the company's new location.

Rudolph will guide our move

from One World Trade Center

to Two World Trade Center

Happy Holidays!

MANCINI·DUFFY

Design Firm
Shamlian Advertising

Art Director
Fred Shamlian

Designers
Fred Shamlian, Stephen Bagi

Original Size
6" x 6" (15 cm x 15 cm)

Client
HABA, Japan

Purpose/Occasion
Promotional holiday calendar

Printing
4-color lithography

Alberta Cosmetics of Tokyo, Japan turned to Shamlian Advertising to produce an inexpensive, spiral-bound calendar for distribution to its customers, employees, and vendors. When a spiral binding proved too expensive, the firm chose this format, which features Alberta's pine tree logo as a subtle graphic element throughout. The cards for each month feature photos that would crop well overall, to the edge of the ghosted area and to the perforation. The first card appears unperforated, and gives no hint of what follows—emphasizing the holiday message and creating curiosity about the gift.

Design Firm
Dyer/Mutchnick Group Inc.

Art Director
Rod Dyer

Designer/Illustrator
Hun Wynn

Original Size
7" x 5" (18 cm x 13 cm)

Client
Pane E. Vino

Purpose/Occasion
Christmas invitation

The designer created this Christmas
postcard in Adobe Illustrator.

Designer/Illustrator
Maria Friske

Original Size
4" x 6" (10 cm x 15 cm)

Mixed media painting
which incorporates, among
other things, pàpier-mâché
heads (on the Santas).
The designer created it as
a Christmas card for clients
and family.

Design Firm
Tim Ernst Cartoons

**Art Director/
Designer/
Illustrator**
Tim Ernst

Original Size
4" x 6" (10 cm x 15 cm)

Client
Foreign Buyers' Club Japan

Purpose/Occasion
Holiday greeting cards

Printing
Photo offset

The cards are hand-drawn images with screen tone
and color tone added. The client wanted images
for Christmas cards that used a Japanese setting
with Western-style humor.

Design Firm
Ads To Go Inc.

Art Director/Illustrator
Gary Grasmoen

Designer
Laura Kaplan

Original Size
6" x 4" (15 cm x 10 cm)

Client
Tom Schmidt's Urban Retreat

Printing
1-color

To promote special spa services for Mothers' Day gift-giving, the client wanted to attract attention in a fun, off-beat manner; the business resides in a somewhat upscale but very trendy area. The price promotion was necessary, but executing it in a unique way grabs attention. The art is a photo of Grandma, superimposed with curlers. This very effective promotion generated more than fifteen percent response.

IF YOUR MOTHER EVER EMBARRASSED YOU IN FRONT OF YOUR FRIENDS WITH A FRUMPY HOUSEDRESS, NO MAKEUP & A BUNCH OF CURLERS, GIVE HER A DAY SHE'LL NEVER FORGET.

MOTHER'S DAY SPA RETREAT $89.

Live Your Dream...Alaska!

Book a Princess Alaska Vacation by February 14th and save from $1,100 to $2,400 per couple.

Private First-class Rail Trips

Denali National Park

Spectacular Lodges

Magnificent Scenery

Design Firm
Belyea Design Alliance

Art Director/Designer
Tim Ruszel

Photographers
Michele Barnes, Terry Reed

Original Size
5 1/2" x 9" (14 cm x 23 cm)

Client
Princess Tours

Purpose/Occasion
Valentine Cruise: Love Boat

Laid out in QuarkXPress, this postcard features logos and photos built and manipulated in Adobe Illustrator and Photoshop. Its purpose was to entice people to book early Alaska cruises at a special discounted rate.

WISHING YOU GOOD LUCK IN THE YEAR OF THE RAT

1 9 9 6

z z z z z z

Design Firm
Ken Weightman Design

**Art Director/
Designer/
Illustrator**
Ken Weightman

Original Size
4" x 5 1/2" (10 cm x 13 cm)

Printing
Laser

The designer used this card as a self-promotion piece, sent at New Year's to clients and friends. The front comes printed on colored paper; the back is customized with a message and mounted to the front. The yellow splotch was added with a copy color heat transfer.

Design Firm
Super Stock Inc.

Creative Concept/Copywriter
Kristine Mangini

Art Director
Kim Sailers

Photographer/Special Effects
SuperStock Vintage Collection

Original Size
7" x 5" (18 cm x 13 cm)

Printing
2-color/duotone

Title
"Research Fees Are For Turkeys"

The stock-photo agency used this research/service-fee promotion created in QuarkXPress in an effort to increase calls by omitting fees. The promotion lasted through Thanksgiving; the free gift was a phone card worth 20 minutes of free long-distance—a perfect way to get the client talking about the promotion.

"Research Fees" Are For Turkeys...

Turkey...

Turkey...?

SUPER STOCK

RETAIL
―――――
RESTAURANT

[ties for mo

[ties for money] STYLE A) has letters. STYLE B) has numbers.

Design Firm
Segura Inc.

Designer
Carlos Segura

Original Size
6" x 9" (15 cm x 23 cm)

Client
[T-26]

This card promotes a limited-edition silk tie designed by Marc Hauser for [T-26].

JOURNEY IN THE MIDDLE OF THE ROAD

One Woman's Path Through a Midlife Education

Muriel Murch

Design Firm
Design Studio Selby

Designer
Robert Selby

Original Size
6" x 4" (15 cm x 10 cm)

Client
Sibyl Publications Inc.

Purpose/Occasion
Publicity for new book

Printing
Offset lithography

These cards served as mailings and hand-outs for *Journey in the Middle of the Road*. There's space for overprinting late-breaking news on the back side (e.g., "Available at __", "Listed one of top 10 books of 1995").

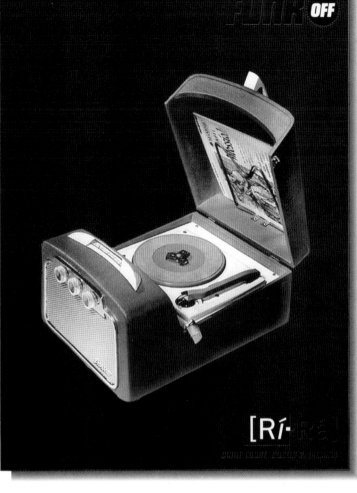

Design Firm
Dynamo

Art Director/Designer
Brian Nolan

Original Size
6" x 4" (15 cm x 10 cm)

Client
Rí-Rá

This flyer for Rí-Rá—
a nightclub that features a
different musical theme
each night—was designed
in Illustrator, using some
Adobe Photoshop imagery.

104A

please mind your handbag

Design Firm
Art Chantry

Art Director/Designer
Art Chantry

Original Size
8" x 4 1/2" (20 cm x 11 cm)

Client
Estrus Records

Printing
Offset

A record release promotional for The Mortals' fake spy movie soundtrack called *Bulletproof* comes with a hole drilled in the center of the gun barrel.

Design Firm
Dynamo

Art Director/Designer
Brian Nolan

Original Size
6" x 4" (15 cm x 10 cm)

Client
Rí-Rá

A flyer for a nightclub event called called "Strictly Handbag"—part of a continuing series of various pop-out-and-make handbags—gives you something to do while thinking about where to go. Designed in Adobe Illustrator, using Photoshop imagery.

Design Firm
Sayles Graphic Design

Art Director/Designer
John Sayles

Original Size
5 1/2" x 9" (14 cm x 23 cm)

Client
The Pier

Purpose/Occasion
Promotion

Printing
Offset

In this postcard series, designer John Sayles takes a humorous approach to illustrating some of this seafood restaurant's most popular dishes. The designer used special effects such as thermography and foil-stamping on select versions to add emphasis.

Design Firm
Art Chantry

Art Director/Designer
Art Chantry

Original Size
4 1/2" x 6" (11 cm x 15 cm)

Client
Estrus Records

Printing
Offset

A general promotional card
for the Estrus record label.

Design Firm
Art Chantry

Art Director/Designer
Art Chantry

Original Size
5 1/2" x 4" (14 cm x 10 cm)

Client
The Rocket

Printing
Offset

The client is a free, monthly
music tabloid in the Seattle
area; the card is part of a
monthly mailing to remind
advertisers that ad deadlines
are approaching.

Design Firm
Segura Inc.

Art Director/Designer
Carlos Segura

Illustrators
Tony Klassen,
Jon Ritter, Mark Rattin

Original Size
9" x 6" (23 cm x 15 cm)

Client
[T-26]

Purpose/Occasion
Promote and generate sales

This card promotes a new font
released by Carlos Segura
called "Time in Hell."

Designer
Sharon DeLaCruz

Quilter/Artist
Sharon DeLaCruz

Photographer
James Smestad

Original Size
4" x 5" (10 cm x 13 cm)

Printing

Lithography

For weeks, the quilter/artist stood by
the lakefront awaiting the correct weather
factors: a perfect gust of wind and
proper sunlight. Finally, the quilt edges
aligned precisely with the horizon lines.
The card promotes the quilt, which required
2,000 hours of hand-stitching to complete.

Design Firm
Dynamo

Art Director/Designer
Brian Nolan

Original Size
6" x 4" (15 cm x 10 cm)

Purpose/Occasion
Nightclub promotion

Client
Strictly Fish

This flyer for a nightclub called "Strictly Fish"—various fishy topics form part of an ongoing theme—was designed in Adobe Illustrator.

Design Firm
Area-Strategic Design

Art Director
Antonio Romano

Designer
Francesca Monrosi

Photographer
Giuseppe Fadda

Client
Giki

Purpose/Occasion
Shoe Sale

Printing
Lithography

This card shows the convenience in buying during the sale season without using prices or any reference to money.

Design Firm
Rosenworld

Art Director
Georgia Christensen

Designer/Illustrator
Laurie Rosenwald

Original Size
6" x 4" (15 cm x 10 cm)

Client
Neiman Marcus

Neiman Marcus created a card for each department of its stores. Shown are the cards for the childrens', housewares, millinery, and holiday departments.

Design Firm
Britches of Georgetowne

Art Director/Designer
Suzanne McCallum

Illustrator
Kevin Pope

Original Size
7 1/2" x 5 1/2" (19 cm x 14 cm)

Client
Britches of Georgetowne

Printing
4-color process

Britches of Georgetowne sent
this postcard in a direct-mail
campaign to reactivate clients
who had not shopped at
the store for several months.

Design Firm
Future Studio

**Art Director/
Designer/
Client**
Amy Inouye

Original Size
5 1/2" x 4" (14 cm x 10 cm)

Photographer
Andy Caulfield

Printing
4-color lithography

Created as a promotional piece for
the studio, this card also promotes
the firm's "other" business—
the "Chicken Boy" catalog
mail-order company that hawks
pop-culture gift items.

Design Firm
Marcolina Design Inc.

Art Director
Daniel Marcolina

Designer/Illustrator
Sean McCabe

Original Size
4" x 6" (10 cm x 15 cm)

Client
Letraset

Printing
Digital printing

Introduction of Letraset's royalty-free CD-ROM image collections in its Photo CD Series; the designer created the card with Adobe Photoshop and Illustrator, as well as Specular Collage.

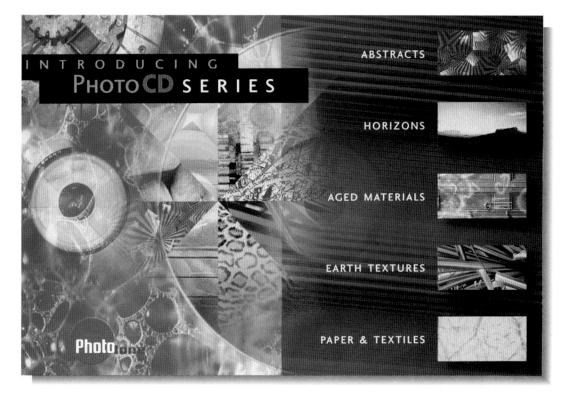

Design Firm
Art Chantry

Art Director/Designer
Art Chantry

Original Size
7 1/2" x 4 1/2" (19 cm x 11 cm)

Client
The Rocket

Printing
Offset

The client is a free music tabloid monthly in the Seattle area; the card is one of a monthly series that reminds advertisers that ad placement deadlines are approaching.

Design Firm
Bartels & Company

Art Director/Designer
David Bartels

Illustrator
Terry Speer

Original Size
9" x 6" (23 cm x 15 cm)

Client
Sinclairs American Grill

Purpose/Occasion
Restaurant premium

Printing
4-color lithography

This fanciful postcard reflects the theme of the Florida restaurant, which gave away the postcard free for the asking. Artist Terry Speer painted the brightly illustrated beach dogs using watercolors.

Design Firm
Shamlian Advertising

Art Director
Fred Shamlian

Designers
Fred Shamlian, Stephen Bagi

Illustrator
Heidi Stevens

Photographer
Walter Plotnik

Original Size
5 1/2" x 7 1/2" (14 cm x 19 cm)

Client
Bravo Bistro

Purpose/Occasion
Wave mailing to attract customers

Printing
4-color lithography

Bravo Bistro, a casual and stylish restaurant on Philadelphia's "Main Line," attracts a young, professional crowd. Because Bravo's patrons say that the waiters and bartenders are what makes their dining special, they were featured in the campaign. The designer brought the art and photography together with the computer.

Design Firm
Design Factory

Art Director/Designer
Conor Clarke

Original Size
4" x 6" (10 cm x 15 cm)

Client
"Haus" the Design Store

Purpose/Occasion
Promotion

Printing
Offset lithography

Much of the design principles for "Haus" the Design Store come from the teachings of original Bauhaus masters, particularly Herbert Bayer. The typography on this card used original fonts redrawn by "The Foundry" in London, Architype Bayer and Architype Renner, assembled in QuarkXPress.

Design Firm
Hilton International, Bangkok

Designer
Prasart Sirimong Yol

Original Size
4 1/2" x 7 1/2" (12 cm x 19 cm)

Client
Hilton International, Bangkok

Purpose/Occasion
Promotional material

Printing
150 gsm art paper, laminated both sides, die-cut

The die-cut emphasizes the Jigsaw design; the concept is a contrast of color that stresses the message.

burning times

rumors of the big wave

"I spent the warmth of my spirit in the wasteland 'til the wasteland blossomed."

from *Spirit in the Wasteland* by Charlie Murphy

Design Firm
Art Chantry

Art Director/Designer
Art Chantry

Illustrator
Gary Sorenson

Original Size
4" x 6" (10 cm x 15 cm)

Client
Rumors of the Big Wave

Printing
Offset

A record release promotional for the record *Burning Times* by Rumors of the Big Wave.

CHARACTERS
BY
BILL NELSON
107 East Cary Street
Richmond, VA 23219

Design Firm
Bill Nelson Illustration Inc.

Art Director/ Designer/ Sculptor
Bill Nelson

Photographer
Tim Gabbert

Original Size
8 1/2" x 6" (22 cm x 15 cm)

Printing
Offset

Depicted on the card is a three-dimensional sculpture of a man in a white shirt and a plaid tie that advertises one-of-a-kind art dolls.

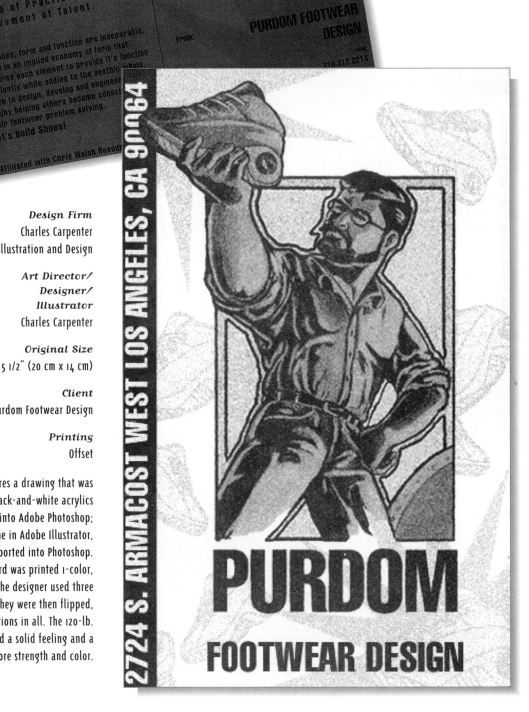

Design Firm
Charles Carpenter
Illustration and Design

**Art Director/
Designer/
Illustrator**
Charles Carpenter

Original Size
8" x 5 1/2" (20 cm x 14 cm)

Client
Purdom Footwear Design

Printing
Offset

The obverse features a drawing that was painted over with black-and-white acrylics and scanned into Adobe Photoshop; the reverse was done in Adobe Illustrator, and the artwork imported into Photoshop. To save money, the card was printed 1-color, in large quantity. The designer used three types of duplexes; they were then flipped, creating six variations in all. The 120-lb. stock gives the card a solid feeling and a little more strength and color.

Design Firm
Segura Inc.

**Art Director/
Designer/
Illustrator**
Carlos Segura

Original Size
9" x 6" (23 cm x 15 cm)

Client
Gimcracks

Purpose/Occasion
Sales promotion

Printing
2-color

This card promotes a store
selling "organic" pieces of
art for the home.

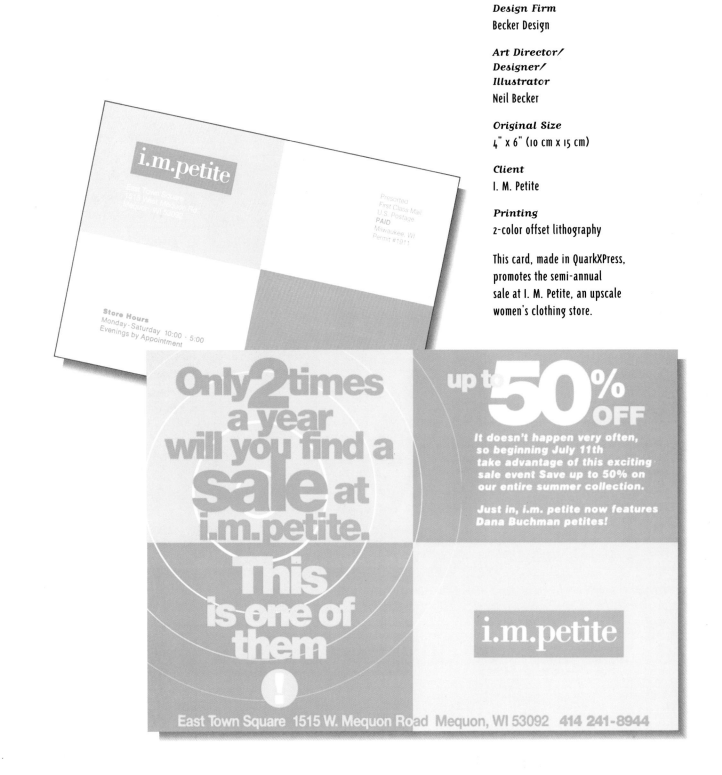

Design Firm
Becker Design

Art Director/
Designer/
Illustrator
Neil Becker

Original Size
4" x 6" (10 cm x 15 cm)

Client
I. M. Petite

Printing
2-color offset lithography

This card, made in QuarkXPress, promotes the semi-annual sale at I. M. Petite, an upscale women's clothing store.

Summer delights
from Chocolate Lace

Ah, summer...
porch swings, picnics and warm breezes

Light, refreshing cakes from Chocolate Lace are always a great way to dress up a party table. New this season are Patio & Picnic Brownie Trays, featuring a complete selection of Gail's favorite brownie recipes, and Cool Lime Torte, a light cheese-cake with a refreshing lime flavor.

For your summer entertaining, be sure to start your party planning with Chocolate Lace.

NEW! PATIO & PICNIC ASSORTMENT TRAYS
For summer entertaining

A delicious variety of bite-sized gourmet pecan squares and brownies — white and dark chocolate, walnut, cappuccino, turtle and white chocolate. Twenty half-sized pieces on a rattan serving tray. Ready for packing in the picnic basket.

FLAG CAKE
Celebrate Independence Day in a sweet way

Yellow sponge cake topped with fresh blueberries and strawberries. A light and delightful salute to summer.

NEW! COOL LIME TORTE
Sweet Summer Sensation

Tall, light cheesecake, with a butter-cookie crust, cream cheese and marsh-mallow cream filling, topped with candy lime slices and whipped cream.

BERRY BASKET CAKE
Held over by popular demand

Perfect for special occasions — birthdays, anniversaries or retirements — when a regular cake won't do. A light chocolate sponge cake, filled with cocoa cream, decorated with Swiss chocolate frosting, and topped with strawberries, raspber-ries, blackberries or blueberries.

COMING IN SEPTEMBER

APPLE BAVARIAN
Zesty treat signals start of fall

A winning combination of creamy cheese-cake and strudel with the unbeatable taste of fresh apples.

Enjoy a delicious dessert break at one of our outdoor umbrella tables.

762.0402

Chocolate Lace 53rd & John Deere Rd., Moline

Hours: Tues.-Sat. 10 a.m. to 5 p.m. WE'LL BE OPEN MONDAY, JULY 3RD FROM 12 P.M. TO 5 P.M.

Chocolate Lace
5202 38th Avenue
Moline, Illinois 61265

Enjoy Chocolate Lace gourmet desserts at your next picnic, pool or patio party.

Design Firm
Gackel Anderson Henningsen Inc.

**Art Director/
Designer/
Illustrator**
Wendy Anderson

Original Size
8" x 6" (20 cm x 15 cm)

Client
Chocolate Lace

Purpose/Occasion
Summer specials

Printing
1-color offset

The designer used Photoshop for the images and QuarkXPress for the layout. The look of summer was created—nice, warm colors to express the time of year. The postcard was successful in bringing people in for the specials.

Design Firm
Belyea Design Alliance

Art Director/Designer
Adrianna Jumping Eagle

Photographer
Roger Schreiber

Original Size
6" x 4" (15 cm x 10 cm)

Client
The Glass Eye

Printing
Offset

The designer created this Christmas-sale postcard in QuarkXPress, importing photos—provided by the client—from Photoshop. The postcard reminds customers to increase the client's Christmas sales.

OG120
Cranberry & White Ribbon

OG123
Blue & White Ribbon

OG110
Ruby with Murrini

THE GLASS EYE ELVES
ARE STILL SHIPPING
IN 10 WORKING DAYS (OR LESS)!

SELF-PROMOTION

Design Firm
Elmwood

Designer
James Backhurst

Original Size
4" x 6" (10 cm x 15 cm)

Elmwood created a range of postcards for both self-promotion and as compliment slips. The images on the postcards come from samples of the firm's work.

design

YORKSHIRE WATER
corporate literature by ELMWOOD

Design Firm
Insight Design Communications

**Art Director/
Designer/
Illustrator**
Tracy and Sherrie Holdeman

Original Size
6" x 5" (15 cm x 13 cm)

Client
AIGA, Wichita Chapter

Printing
Indigo press

This piece was the cover of a mailer for an AIGA/Wichita Macintosh workshop. It was done entirely in Adobe Photoshop, depicting a funky computer screen, keyboard, and mouse in a woodsy, "workshop-like" style. The designer scanned elements from '50s do-it-yourself books. In the bottom left-hand corner, the designer scanned type with more pertinent copy.

Design Firm
Richard Puder Design

Art Director
Richard Puder

Designer
Lee Grabarczyk

Illustrators
Nina La Den [above];
Lori Anzalone, Judith Mitchell
[opposite page]

Original Size
6" x 11" (15 cm x 28 cm)

Printing
2-color; 3-color

Titled "Postcards From Dover No. 16,"
[above] and "Postcards From Dover
No. 10" [opposite page], this series
was created in Macromedia FreeHand,
with copy joined to paths. The series
creatively identifies the firm's
location and underlines what it
offers in design.

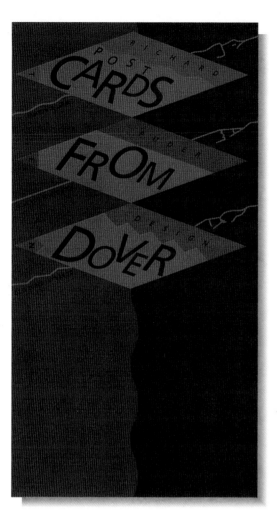

Design Firm
Elmwood

Designer
James Backhurst

Original Size
6" x 4" (15 cm x 10 cm)

Elmwood created a range of postcards for both self-promotion and as compliment slips. The images on the postcards come from samples of the firm's work.

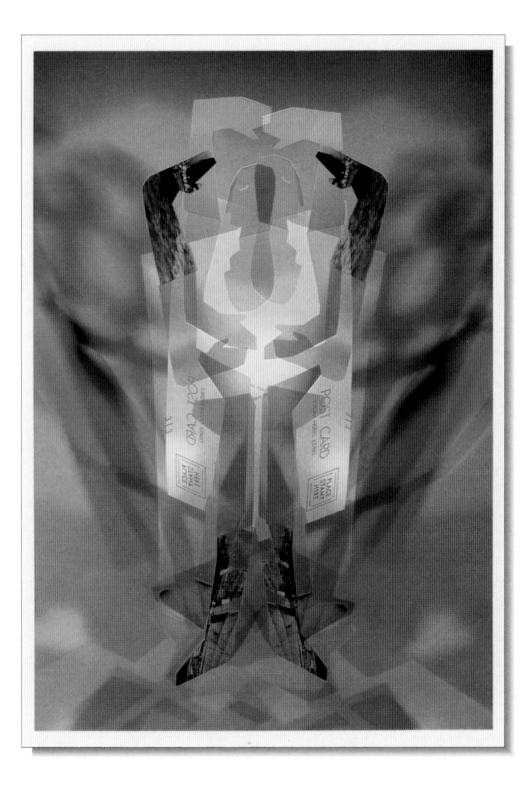

Design Firm
Kan Tai-keung Design
& Associates Ltd.

Art Director/Designer
Freeman Lau Siu Hong

Original Size
7" x 5" (18 cm x 13 cm)

Client
Hong Kong Designers
Association

Photographer
C. K. Wong

This design was a picture of
a human image created by
postcard; therefore, the design
firm named it "a postcard
posed a pose for post."

Design Firm
Schudlich Design & Illustration

Art Director/ Designer/ Illustrator
Stephen Schudlich

Photographer
Jon Bruton

Original Size
4" x 8" (10 cm x 20 cm)

Client
Ceci Bartels Associates

Purpose/Occasion
Raincheck promotion

Printing
4-color lithography

This program created an easy and systematic way of establishing awareness for the agency. It enabled agents to more easily get appointments and provided a consistent message all the way to the follow-through after the appointment.

Remember to Contact...

Johnson, West & Company

1400 Pioneer Building
336 Robert Street North
St. Paul, MN 55101-1546

BULK RATE
U.S. POSTAGE
PAID
Permit No. 2744
St. Paul, MN

Are you gambling with your organizations license?

Let Johnson
West keep
you **covered!**

Call! Johnson, West & Company,
Certified Public Accountants
(612) 227-9431--Ask for Steve Miller.

Design Firm
Design Center

Art Director
John Reger

Designer
Sherwin Schwartzrock

Original Size
6" x 4" (15 cm x 10 cm)

Client
Johnson, West & Company

Printing
4-color offset

Instead of designing a straight-forward, serious promotion, the designer decided upon something very colorful and fun, not typical for certified public accountants. The client loved the approach.

Designer/Illustrator
Ulana Zahajkewycz

Original Size
6" x 8 1/2" (15 cm x 22 cm)

This postcard, gouache on watercolor paper, reflects the artist's wacky style. "Speeding Dog" looks nutty, but that's exactly the reaction the artist wanted—fun, fun, fun.

Design Firm
Dragon's Teeth Design

Designer/Illustrator
Greg Hricenak

Original Size
4" x 6" (10 cm x 15 cm)

Purpose/Occasion
Annual promotional package

Printing
Offset

This card features a pen and ink (crow quill pen) drawing that was scanned and imported into QuarkXPress.

Design Firm
Free-Range Chicken Ranch

Art Director
Toni Parmley

Designer/Illustrator
Kelli Christman

Photographer
Jack Christianson

Original Size
4 1/2" x 6" (11 cm x 15 cm)

Printing
Offset

When an opportunity to get a lot of postcards printed at a discount price came up, this self-promotional card was born. To tie in the chicken theme, the Ranch used real live chickens as models. In processing, the film was damaged; it took 2–3 photos and Adobe Photoshop work to recreate the scene.

Art Director
Dennis Irwin

Designer/Illustrator
Dennis Irwin

Original Size
5" x 7 1/2" (13 cm x 19 cm)

The designer created this photo collage with a gluestick and his favorite scissors, the Swiss Army knife scissors. The hungry dog symbolizes who else but the hungry illustrator.

Design Firm
XJR Design

Designer
Roger Foin

Illustrator
Da Vinci

Original Size
4" x 5 1/2" (10 cm x 14 cm)

Client
Da Vinci

Printing
1-color lithography

This mailing promotes the firm's work for a popular Italian restaurant.

PACKAGING & VISUAL COMMUNICATIONS

700 N. Green Street • Chicago, IL 60622
312-243-3377 • FAX: 312-243-8947

XJR design LLP

Old world quality, design and illustrations for line of gourmet deli cheeses conceived and executed by studio principal, including logo and classic botanical style illustrations.

Design Firm
After Hours Creative

Original Size
5" x 8" (13 cm x 20 c m)

Printing
Rubber stamp

Sent to all After Hours clients and vendors, this card let them know that the design firm was in temporary quarters until its new office space was completed. Because the firm totally forgot about sending an announcement about its temporary space until they were actually in it, the firm simply tore up moving boxes, made some stamps, and sent the card out.

design as an instrument of increasing happiness ☺

Design Firm
Elmwood

Designer
James Backhurst

Original Size
6" x 4" (15 cm x 10 cm)

Elmwood created a range of postcards for both self-promotion and as compliment slips. The images on the postcards come from samples of the firm's work.

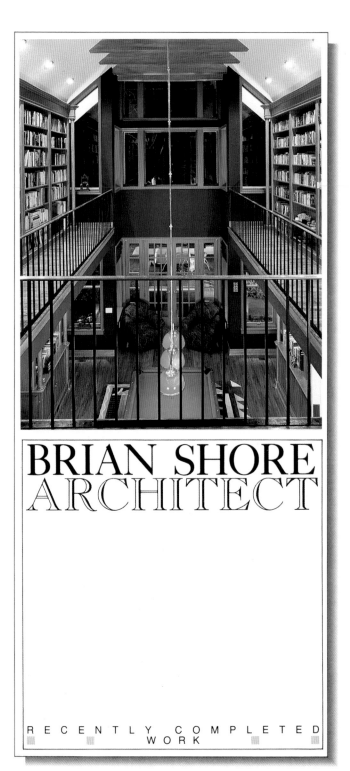

OH BOY

CAN YOU HELP REGGIE ROACH GET TO THE PASTRAMI SANDWICH?

Art Director/
Designer/
Illustrator
Marc Rosenthal

Original Size
6" x 4 1/2" (15 cm x 11 cm)

Client
Gerald & Cullen Rapp Inc.

Printing
4-color process

This ink-and-watercolor piece came out of the designer's drawing puzzles and mazes for his 8-year-old son.

Design Firm
Brian Shore, Architect

Art Director
Sally Shore

Designer
Brian Shore

Photographer
Various

Original Size
9" x 4" (23 cm x 10 cm)

Printing
Offset lithography

The architect mails a single card to past and potential clients every four months to foster awareness of Shore's practice, and to demonstrate to all the range of work produced.

BRIAN SHORE ARCHITECT

RECENTLY COMPLETED WORK

**Art Director/
Designer/
Illustrator**
James Steinberg

Original Size
6" x 4" (15 cm x 10 cm)

Client
Gerald & Cullen Rapp Inc.

Printing
4-color process

This card draws upon various symbols in the designer's inventory.

Rebecca Grimes Illustration
(410) 857-1675

**Art Director/
Designer/
Illustrator**
Rebecca Grimes

Original Size
6" x 4" (15 cm x 10 cm)

Photographer
Robert Porterfield

Printing
Offset lithography

The artist created this dimensional illustration titled "Vegetable Gothic"—a takeoff on Grant Wood's *American Gothic*—using Polyform (clay) and fabric. The sculpture was mounted on 1/4" (0.6 cm) foamcore board and framed. Photographed as a 4" x 5" (10 cm x 13 cm) transparency.

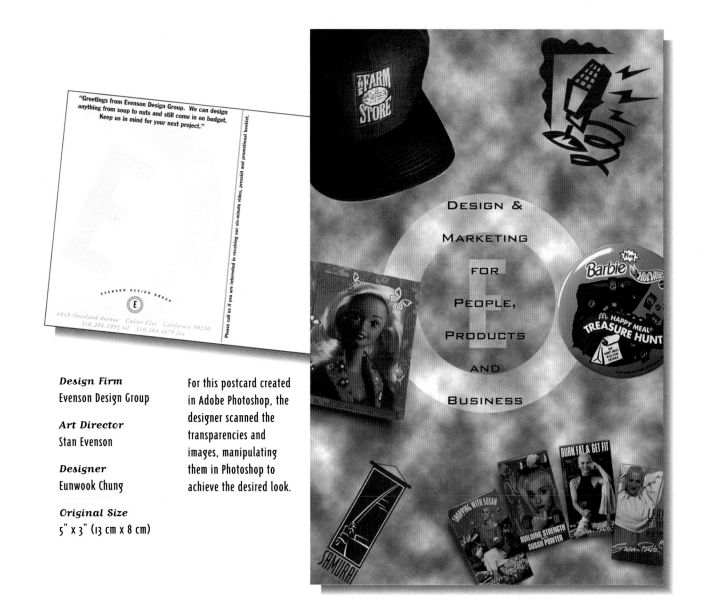

Design Firm
Evenson Design Group

Art Director
Stan Evenson

Designer
Eunwook Chung

Original Size
5" x 3" (13 cm x 8 cm)

For this postcard created in Adobe Photoshop, the designer scanned the transparencies and images, manipulating them in Photoshop to achieve the desired look.

Design Firm
Fordesign

Art Director/Designer/Typographer
Frank Ford

Photographer
Susan Peylon, Macropho

Original Size
5 1/2" x 8" (14 cm x 20 cm)

Printing
2-color metallic duotone with foil stamp

With a $1,000 budget, the designer initially created the card as a promotion for his "Stroke" font, which is very expressionistic. The excess cards sold at a fine-art specialty gift shop on consignment and as postcards. The designer converted the background image of the birds into a duotone in Adobe Photoshop that was motion-blurred and fragmented; the type was pinched and twirled in Adobe Illustrator.

Design Firm
David Bamundo Illustration

Designer/Illustrator
David Bamundo

Original Size
6" x 4" (15 cm x 10 cm)

Created with Adobe Illustrator, this multi-purpose card features four illustrations together to make a postcard mailer with the help of a large shipping label on the black-and-white side. Cut into four pieces, it becomes four business cards.

Designer/Photographer
Kevin Bond

Original Size
5 1/2" x 7" (14 cm x 18 cm)

This card for a Chinese lingerie company in Hong Kong began with a black-and-white photo, colored in Adobe Photoshop. The artist designed the type in Illustrator after scanning the Kanji characters, and imported the type into Photoshop, later placing it in QuarkXPress. After the fact, the store discovered that the Chinese government wouldn't allow this logo because it uses a real flower, so it used the card in Hong Kong.

Design Firm
Cindy Wrobel, Design & Illustration

**Art Director/
Designer/
Illustrator**
Cindy Wrobel

Original Size
6" x 4" (15 cm x 10 cm)

Printing
Offset

The artist created this card as scratchboard art, then she cut an overlay from amberlith for the second color (orange). She used green ink to hand-color the leaves. The illustrator sent the card to potential clients.

Art Director/
Designer/
Illustrator
Hal Mayforth

Original Size
6" x 4" (15 cm x 10 cm)

Client
Gerald & Cullen Rapp Inc.

Printing
4-color process

Living in Vermont and having mountain views through his studio windows, the designer offers up-to-date ski conditions as a fringe benefit to clients.

Design Firm
Mixed Nuts Inc.

Art Director/
Designer
Bill Boyko

Original Size
6" x 4" (15 cm x 10 cm)

Printing
4-color

Created with airbrush, gouache, and pencil, this card promotes realism technique as well as the launch of a new artist rep.

Design Firm
Bethanie Deeney Illustration

**Art Director/
Designer/
Illustrator**
Bethanie Deeney

This is a self-promotional postcard
specifically advertising spot illustrations.
The designer created the black outlines of
the illustrations, as well as the funky text
in Illustrator. The illustrator colored the
cards by hand with Luma dyes.

Design Firm
Visible Ink

Designer/Illustrator
Sharon Howard Constant

Original Size
5" x 7" (13 cm x 18 cm)

Printing
4-color process over black

Title
"Frog Prince"

Original drawing done entirely in CorelDraw using fractal fills to "paint" the background. Type treatment for "Change" was done in Adobe Photoshop using Alien Skin drop shadow and glass filters. Layout, prepress, and separations were done in CorelDraw.

Are you looking for a **Change?**

BETHANIE DEENEY

(212)780-4830

254 Park Avenue South, Suite 4M
New York, NY 10010

ILLUST

Design Firm
Bethanie Deeney Illustration

Art Director/ Designer/ Illustrator
Bethanie Deeney

Original Size
4" x 6" (10 cm x 15 cm)

The postcard is a self-promotion piece for an illustration business. The design was done in QuarkXPress, the bear dingbat created in Adobe Illustrator, and the illustrations done by hand in watercolor.

Design Firm
Paul Stoddard Illustration

**Art Director/
Designer/
Illustrator**
Paul Stoddard

Original Size
8" x 4 1/2" (20 cm x 11 cm)

The designer created this promotional to target the book publisher market. The Three Bears illustration's original size was 11" x 11" (28 cm x 28 cm), its media ink, watercolor, and color pencil. The illustration from the poem by Robert Louis Stevenson "My Bed is a Boat" was originally drawn at 7" x 13" (18 cm x 33 cm), its media ink, watercolor, and color pencil.

Design Firm
Cindy Wrobel, Design & Illustration

**Art Director/
Designer/
Illustrator**
Cindy Wrobel

Original Size
6" x 4" (15 cm x 10 cm)

Printing
1-color offset, hand-colored

The artist made this scratchboard art, done on location in Provence, into a self-promotional postcard in 1994. After printing, she hand-colored the piece with colored pencil. The card was sent out as part of a client mailing/ self-promotional postcard series.

OR JUST
CALL US.

(510) 836-484

Visible Ink
Graphic Design • Illustration
678 13th Street, Suite 202
Oakland, CA 94612

HOURS OF PAINSTAKING WORK…

YEARS OF TECHNICAL STUDY…

GENERATIONS OF KNOWLEDGE…

CENTURIES OF CLOSELY
GUARDED SECRETS…

Design Firm
Visible Ink

Designer
Sharon Howard Constant

Original Size
5" x 7" (13 cm x 18 cm)

Printing
4-color process over black

Title
"Kimono"

Created entirely in CorelDraw with extensive use of the layers function to manage the thousands of objects. Prepress and separations also done in CorelDraw.

Design Firm
C. Carp Designs

Art Director
Carolyn Carpenter

Original Size
6" x 4" (15 cm x 10 cm)

Titled "My Grevy's Zebra," this card is geared toward the licensing market. A Prismacolor pencil drawing from a series titled "All Species Are Endangered Species" depicts endangered animals and plants. Most of the forty or more drawings in the series incorporate nature quotes in the artwork; the quote in the border of "My Grevy's Zebra" is from Henry Beston.

© **CAROLYN CARPENTER** 1994

Design Firm
Standard Deluxe Inc.

Art Director/Designer
William M. Abel, III

Original Size
4 1/2" x 6" (11 cm x 15 cm)

Printing
Silk screen and rubber stamp

The type and truck are hand-drawn,
scanned, and manipulated using
Adobe Illustrator and Streamline;
the Extrude filter created the
compound path of the shadows.

Design Firm
Standard Deluxe Inc.

Art Director
Scott Peek

Designer
Scott Peek/William Abel

Original Size
4" x 6" (10 cm x 15 cm)

Photographer
Lee Isaacs

Printing
Offset lithography

Design Firm
Tieken Design & Creative Services

Art Director
Fred E. Tieken

Designers
Rik Boberg, Fred E. Tieken

Original Size
8 1/2" x 5 1/2" (22 cm x 14 cm)

Purpose/Occasion
Web site announcement

Printing
4-color process and UV coating

The designer used Adobe Photoshop, Adobe Illustrator, and QuarkXPress to create this postcard. The road image was a CD-ROM photo that was manipulated, colorized, and transformed to achieve a photographic negative effect. "Tieken guy" was placed into the road sign and then embedded into the road image; the white center lines in the road were left white to lead the reader to the firm's Web site address. The designer layered the Tieken script logotype in Photoshop to achieve a transparent watermark.

Designer/Illustrator
Brian Cronin

Original Size
6" x 4" (15 cm x 10 cm)

Printing
Offset

A Christmas card for 1995 titled "Stay Warm," the illustration depicts a cone of wool and a person wearing a new sweater, both in green.

WILDFLOWERS IN BLOOM

DESERT BOTANICAL GARDEN

Design Firm
After Hours Creative

Photographer
Art Holeman

Original Size
5" x 7" (13 cm x 18 cm)

Client
Desert Botanical Garden

Printing
Offset lithography

The Desert Botanical Garden mailed this series of postcards to its members, informing them of special upcoming events. The bold, exciting, and unusual cards reflect the bold, exciting events cards promoted. The printer did the cards all at one time to make the 4-color process affordable. Backs were imprinted later in one or two colors, once event information was confirmed.

SPRING PLANT SALE

SALE

DESERT BOTANICAL GARDEN

Design Firm
Honblue Inc.

Original Size
4" x 5" (10 cm x 13 cm)

Printing
Indigo press

This series features some famous
(and some soon-to-be-famous)
photographers strutting their stuff.

Design Firm
Honblue Inc.

Original Size
4" x 5" (10 cm x 13 cm)

Printing
Indigo press

With seven days to get seven designers to create seven postcards, these cards were made reality on the E-Print, a short-run color press that helps keep costs down on limited budgets.

Design Firm
Bartels & Company

Art Director
David Bartels

Designer
Bob Thomas

Illustrators
Montoliu, Wright, Rodriguez, Probert, Pope, Burnett, Lyons, Porfirio

Original Size
Various

Client
Ceci Bartels Associates

Printing
4-color lithography

Ceci Bartels Associates produced this postcard series in a large format in order to make a bigger impression at the point of receipt. Mailed out over the course of many months, the cards increased the awareness level of the artists and the agency among its clients.

Design Firm
Walker Pinfold Associates
(London Ltd.)

Art Director/Designer
Katie Jagger

Illustrator
Debbie Heald

Photographer
Gill Orsman

Original Size
6" x 4" (15 cm x 10 cm)

Printing
4-color lithography

The 3-D illustrations of "the elements of design" hang on the mezzanine floor of Walker Pinfold Associates' studio in Islington, London. Originally centerpieces for the studio to communicate to visiting clients the firm's design principles and the standard of creative services it offers, the firm adapted them to postcards. The designer scanned the photographs of the frames, then retouched them in Adobe Photoshop. The typography and graphics were added in Adobe Illustrator. The postcards are a set of four; the firm uses them for correspondence with clients and as glorified "compliment slips."

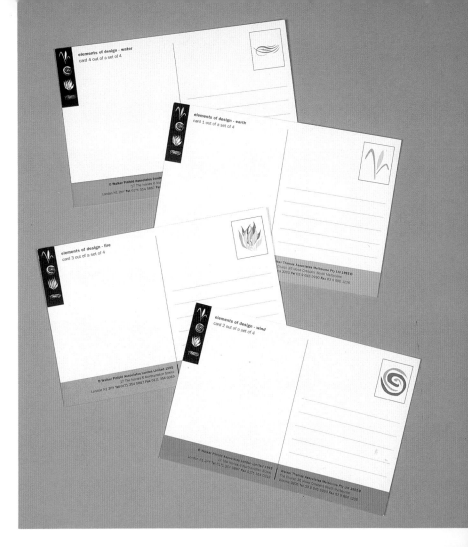

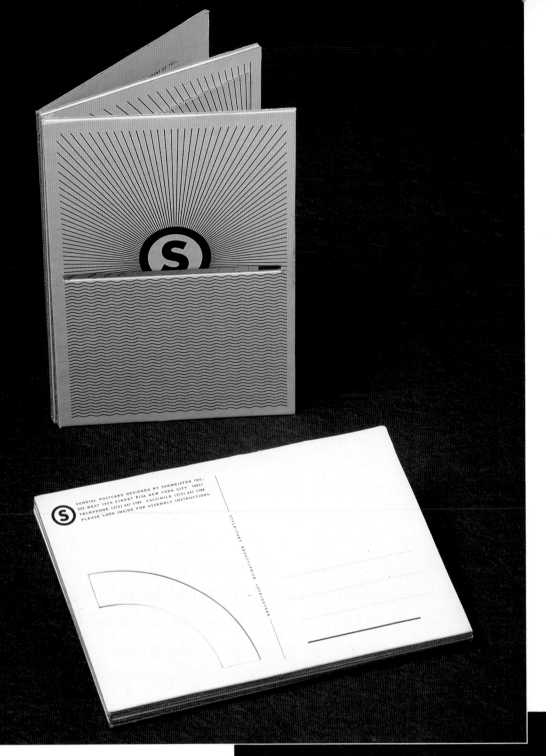

Design Firm
Sagmeister Inc.

Art Director/Designer
Stefan Sagmeister

Illustrator
Veronica Oh

Original Size
6" x 4" (15 cm x 10 cm)

Printing
Offset

This card folds into a real working sundial; the level of the dial adjusts to work in most American cities.

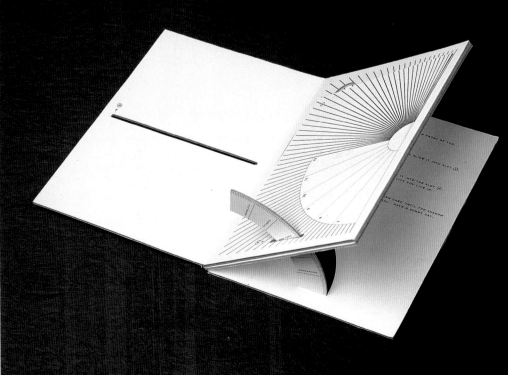

Design Firm
After Hours Creative

Illustrator
Todd Fedell

Photographer
Kevin Cruff

Original Size
9" x 6" (23 cm x 15 cm)

Printing
Offset lithography

Mailed to potential and existing clients, this card informed them that After Hours was opening an office in Atlanta. Clocks are part of the firm's identity system; one clock splitting into two communicates the addition of a second office.

Design Firm
Marcolina Design Inc.

Art Director/ Designer/ Illustrator
Dermot MacCormack

Original Size
4" x 6" (10 cm x 15 cm)

Client
Letraset

Printing
Digital printing

Introduction of Fontek Express service for Letraset using Adobe Photoshop and Illustrator and Specular Collage. The designer used brilliant colors at the client's request for a less formal, more "funky" look.

Design Firm
MGM Illustration

Designer
Gary Pipta

Original Size
4" x 6" (10 cm x 15 cm)

Client/Photographer
Marc Vaughn

This card—assembled in Adobe Photoshop—shows the sense of humor and the ability of the photographer.

Design Firm
Richard Puder Design

Art Director
Richard Puder

Designer/Illustrator
Lee Grabarczyk

Original Size
6" x 18" (15 cm x 46 cm)

Printing
4-color

Titled "Avant Garde," the designer created this piece in Adobe Illustrator and QuarkXPress. Promo gives a brief history of the type and showcases the firm's ability to use it.

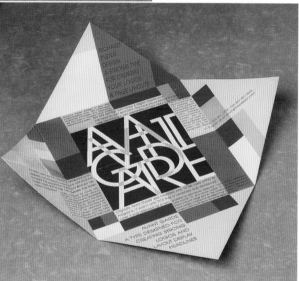

Design Firm
Bartels & Company

Art Director
David Bartels

Designer
Bob Thomas

Illustrators
Montoliu, Wright, Rodriguez, Probert, Pope, Burnett, Lyons, Porfirio

Original Size
5 1/2" x 8 1/2" (14 cm x 21 cm)

Client
Ceci Bartels Associates

Printing
4-color lithography

Ceci Bartels Associates produced this series of cards to increase awareness among art directors of the artists' work. Produced in an oversized format, they stood out more than smaller cards when they hit art directors' desks.

Design Firm
Carole Goodman

Designer/
Illustrator/
Photographer
Carole Goodman

Original Size
8" x 4" (20 cm x 10 cm)

Printing
4-color offset lithography

Tagged onto another job,
this quickly designed piece
is about business, pleasure,
and where the twain meet.

Art Director/Illustrator
Joe Ciardiello

Original Size
4" x 6" (10 cm x 15 cm)

Printing
Offset

Series of postcards mailed to clients
as a mini-portfolio. Various clients
commissioned the artwork—pen and
ink and watercolor illustrations—for
editorial and advertising purposes.

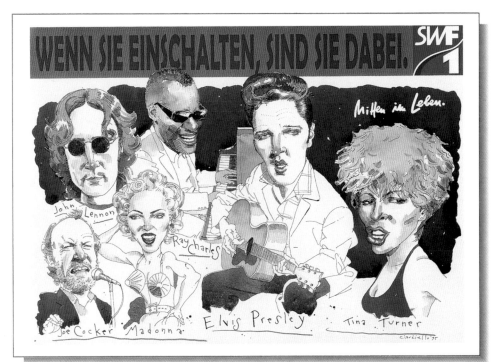

Design Firm
Maverick Art Tribe

**Art Director/
Designer/
Illustrator/Client**
Rick Sealock

Photographer
Mark Mennie

Original Size
4 1/2" x 6 1/2"
(11 cm x 16 cm)

Printing
Offset printing

The type and design had to reflect the same energy and creativity as the illustration(s) used on the cards; this was accomplished with photocopied type, found type and images, and recycling old parts of illustrations.

**Art Director/
Illustrator**
Joe Ciardiello

Original Size
4" x 6" (10 cm x 15 cm)

Printing
Offset

Series of postcards mailed to clients as a mini-portfolio. Various clients commissioned the artwork—pen and ink and watercolor illustrations—for editorial and advertising purposes.

Design Firm
Bartels & Company

Art Director/Designer
David Bartels

Illustrator
Braldt Bralds

Original Size
8 1/2" x 5 1/2" (22 cm x 14 cm)

Printing
4-color lithography

GRAPHIC DESIGN   PACKAGING   SALES PROMOTION

CORPORATE IDENTITY   POSTERS   EVENT MARKETING

A SURE THING   BARTELS & COMPANY   314-781-4350

Design Firm
Thompson Design Group

Art Director
Dennis Thompson

Designer
Mary Sheppard

Original Size
4" x 6" (10 cm x 15 cm)

The purpose of the postcard was to promote new Websites. It used an energetic design strategy featuring Thompson Design Group's identity, as well as package designs developed by Thompson Design.

Design Firm
Mike Salisbury Communications Inc.

Art Director
Mike Salisbury

Designer/Illustrator
Patrick O'Neal

Original Size
9" x 4" (23 cm x 10 cm)

To promote a southern California graphic designer's roots in the California look.

Design Firm
Surburbia Studios

**Art Director/
Designer/
Illustrator**
Jeremie White

Original Size
5 1/2" x 4 1/2" (14 cm x 11 cm)

Client
Jeremie White

Printing
Lithography, four Pantone colors and metallic copper

The illustrations for this two-card set were hand-drawn; the designer created the graphics and type on the Mac with Macromedia FreeHand.

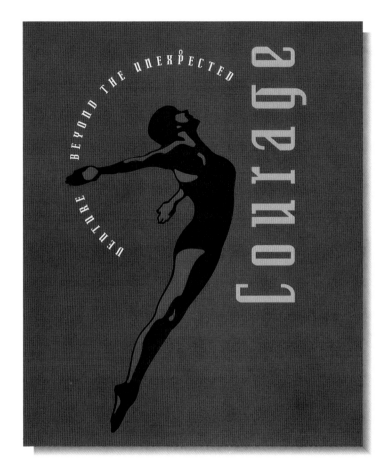

Art Director/
Designer/
Photographer
Gary Krueger

Original Size
3 1/2" x 5 1/2" (9 cm x 14 cm)

Printing
Offset

Design Firm
Clownbank Studio

Art Director/
Designer/
Illustrator
Peter Bartczak

Original Size
9" x 6" (23 cm x 15 cm)

Client
Clownbank Studio

Printing
Offset

TItled "Ballerina," this card
features a limited palette
of airbrushed colors.

Design Firm
Design Center

Art Director
John Reger

Designer
Sherwin Schwartzrock

Original Size
6" x 4" (15 cm x 10 cm)

Client
Johnson, West & Company

Printing
4-color offset

Instead of designing a straightforward, serious promotion, the designer decided upon something very colorful and fun, not typical for certified public accountants. The clients loved the approach.

Design Firm
Troller Assoc.

Art Director/Designer
Fred Troller

Photographer
Beatrice Stoecklin

Original Size
7" x 5" (18 cm x 13 cm)

Client
Alfred University

Printing
Offset

The designer created this piece for a retrospective exhibit honoring his work. The university sent the card to designers and the public interested in art and design.

Design Firm
Richard Puder Design

Art Director
Richard Puder

Designer/Illustrator
Lee Grabarczyk

Original Size
3 1/2" x 18" (9 cm x 46 cm)

Printing
4-color

The designer created this piece, titled "Souvenir," in Adobe Illustrator and QuarkXPress; the card gives a brief history of the typeface and showcases the firm's ability to use it.

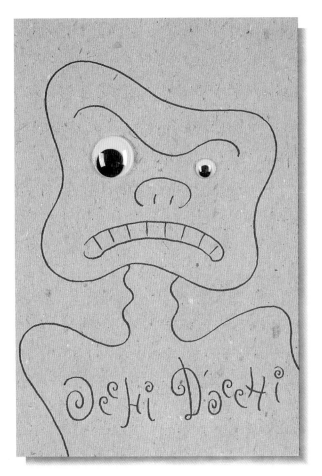

Design Firm
Studio Guarnaccia

**Art Director/
Designer/
Illustrator**
Steven Guarnaccia

Original Size
6" x 4" (15 cm x 10 cm)

Printing
Offset blackline on cardboard, with hand-applied "goggle" eyes.

This card serves as announcement and invitation to a one-person show held at the Affidre Gallery in Milan; the show featured published works and toy-like, three-dimensional pieces by the artist, Steven Guarnaccia. Pronounce the exhibit title, "Occhi D'Occhi" ("Eyes of Eyes"), like "Okey-dokey."

Ignite
new interest in your business

Design Ranch has done just that for so many companies. A shining example is Dadant & Sons, Inc., manufacturers of fine beeswax candles. Design Ranch has helped Dadant strike the perfect match with their customers by creating new

packaging, catalogs and advertisements. The new Dadant logo created by Design Ranch recently won an international award. And now Design Ranch is working with Dadant to develop and market an exciting new consumer product.

DESIGN RANCH

Call 319-354-2623 and see what bright ideas Design Ranch has for you

Design Firm
Design Ranch

Art Director
Gary Gnade

Designer/Copywriter
Kimberly Cooke

Original Size
4 1/2" x 5" (11 cm x 13 cm)

Photographer
Mike Schlotterback,
French Studios

Printing
Offset/blowtorch

Inspired by a client who manufactures candles, this card suggests ways the firm's marketing and design services help "heat up" interest in a client's business. The firm actually burned the edges by hand—with a blowtorch.

Design Firm
Diane Woods

Designer/Illustrator
Diane Woods

Photographer
Ron Maier

Original Size
4" x 6" (10 cm x 15 cm)

Client
Sheridan Avenue Gallery

Used for tourism and souvenirs, the gallery sold this freehand, transparent watercolor painting as single postcards, and also in framed collages of four each.

Design Firm
T.P. Design

Art Directors/Illustrators
Dorothea and Charly Palmer

Original Size
7" x 4 1/2" (18 cm x 11 cm)

Photographers
Marvin Scott, Ernest Washington

Printing
Indigo press

This purpose of this series—created in Adobe Illustrator and Photoshop—was to show different aspects of what T. P. Design has to offer: design, illustration, packaging design, and logos.

Design Firm
Rosenworld

Art Director
Georgia Christensen

Designer/Illustrator
Laurie Rosenwald

Original Size
6" x 4" (15 cm x 10 cm)

Promotional card with chain for nose. Hold the card flat. To create different shapes, shake the card.

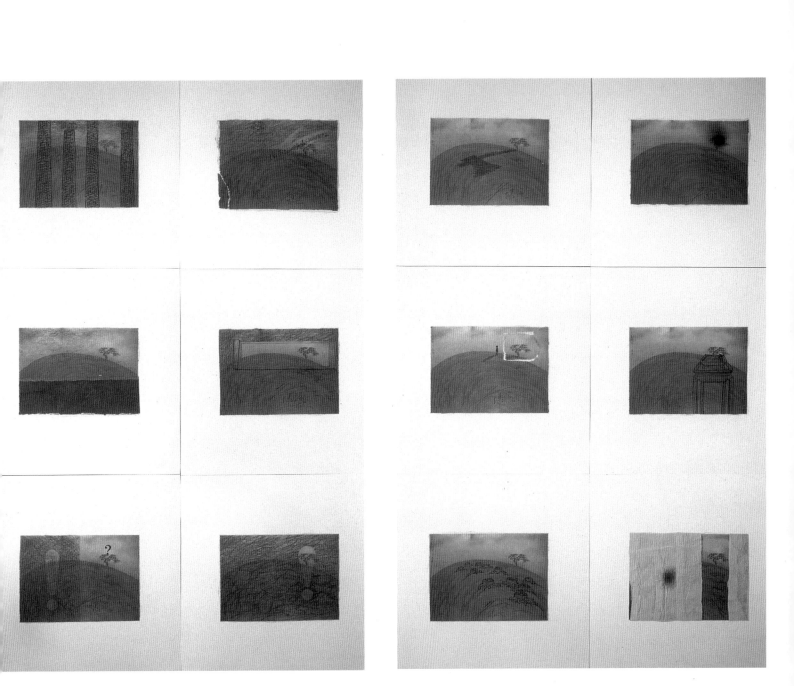

Design Firm
Kan Tai-keung Design &
Associates Ltd.

**Art Director/
Designer/
Illustrator**
Kan Tai-keung

Original Size
4 1/2" x 6" (11 cm x 15 cm)

The designer based this
collection of twelve nature
postcards on a landscape
ink painting.

PHOTOGRAPHY
—————
FINE ART

Art Director/Photographer
Armin Vogt

Original Size
4" x 6" (10 cm x 15 cm)

Client
AVP

These postcards come from a series titled "Sehen" (German for "look"). These images capture various photographs from Italy, France, England, and Switzerland.

Art Director/
Photographer
Armin Vogt

Original Size
4" x 6" (10 cm x 15 cm)

Client
AVP

These postcards come from a series titled "Sehen" (German for "look"). These images capture various photographs from Italy, France, England, and Switzerland.

Design Firm
Chermayeff & Geismar Inc.

**Art Director/
Designer/
Illustrator**
Ivan Chermayeff

Original Size
6" x 4" (15 cm x 10 cm)

Client
Ginza Graphic Gallery

Printing
Offset

The designer made this postcard from a collage for a book on Ivan Chermayeff, and used it as a promotional piece.

Design Firm
Chermayeff & Geismar Inc.

**Art Director/
Designer/
Illustrator**
Ivan Chermayeff

Original Size
4" x 6" (10 cm x 15 cm)

Client
Ginza Graphic Gallery

Purpose/Occasion
Art show promotion

Printing
Offset

The designer created this postcard from a collage showing at the Ginza Graphic Gallery, which used it as a promotional piece.

Design Firm
George Samerjan

Designer
George Samerjan

Original Size
5 1/2" x 8 1/2" (14 cm x 22 cm)

Purpose/Occasion
Samerjan one-man show
retrospective

Printing
Offset

Living in the community for
the past 35 years, the artist
felt that a personal note sent
to people he knew would be
welcome. Instead of the
usual 200 or 300 that visit
the exhibitions, more than a
thousand attended.

Design Firm
So Yoon Lym

**Art Director/
Designer/
Illustrator**
So Yoon Lym

Original Size
5 1/2" x 4" (14 cm x 10 cm)

Purpose/Occasion
Illustrator's promotion

Printing
Color Xerox and ink stamp

Looking for an inexpensive printing process
for an illustration promotional, the illustrator
had a 10" x 12" illustration consisting of 30
different "face" blocks cropped and reduced
on a color Xerox copier, then used a
self-inking stamp made with name, address,
and phone number.

Design Firm
Artbank Editions

Illustrator
James Marsh

Original Size
5" x 6 1/2" (13 cm x 16 cm)

Title
"Fine Filly"

The idea was to create an eye-catching image in a pastiche style, while retaining something of the designer's own style of working.

Designer/ Art Director/ Photographer
Frank Wiedemann

Original Size
5 1/2" x 4" (14 cm x 10 cm)

The photographer created all the images used in this card without the use of a computer; all the work was done on negatives, not in the darkroom printing process.

Design Firm
Big Road Blue

**Art Director/
Designer/
Illustrator**
Tim Davies

Photographer
Laurence Cendrowicz

Original Size
4" x 6" (10 cm x 15 cm)

Client
Tim Davies

Printing
4-color lithography

The illustrator created
the card for self-promotion;
it was given away during
exhibitions of his paintings.
The reverse carried
black-and-white line
drawings of two images;
the obverse shows a recent
painting. It is like a
condensed portfolio!

© **TIM DAVIES** 1994
"3 FIGURES"
ACRYLIC ON CANVAS
100 × 65 cms

CONTACT: ENGLAND
BIG ROAD BLUE STUDIO
66A ELM PARK ROAD
LONDON N3 1EB
TEL: 081-349 3087

CONTACT: REST OF EUROPE
WILFRIED F. RIMENSBURGER
EUROCK STILETTO
ERNSBERGERSTR. 19
D-81241 MÜNCHEN GERMANY
TEL. 089 43664020
FAX. 089 8348816

Design Firm
Dean Johnson Design

Art Director/Illustrator
Bruce Dean

Designer
Scott Johnson

Original Size
4" x 5" (10 cm x 13 cm)

Printing
4-color process

This card showcases Dean
Johnson Design's illustration.

LORRAINE WILLIAMS

ILLUSTRATOR

NEW YORK CITY • FAX AVAILABLE
RSVP CALLBACK ANSWERING SERVICE (718) 857-9267

Design Firm
Lorraine Williams Illustration

**Art Director/
Designer/
Illustrator**
Lorraine Williams

Original Size
8 1/2" x 5 1/2" (21 cm x 14 cm)

Printing
4-color separation

This mixed-media (pastels, watercolor, colored pencils) piece for a concept called "Which wine with fish?" was sent as a general promotion mailer mainly to editorial markets to generate interest in the illustrator's work.

FRAGMENTS OF **EXISTENCE**

NICOLE ANN DESCHAMPS

MASTER OF FINE ARTS
THESIS EXHIBITION

Designer
Kari Payment

Photographer
Cynthia Greig

Original Size
7" x 4" (18 cm x 10 cm)

Client
Nicole DesChamps

Purpose/Occasion
Gallery show

Printing
4-color process

Producer
Augie Ventimiglio

In creating this card, the designer scanned photos of jewelry and retouched them in Adobe Photoshop. The face paintings were placed on the flatbed scanner and scanned directly from art and retouched in Photoshop, then arranged in Photoshop and then exported as a TIFF together as one piece of art, then placed in QuarkXPress. Type set on reverse side was done in QuarkXPress.

Design Firm
Suburbia Studios

**Art Director/
Designer/
Illustrator**
Russ Willms

Original Size
4 1/2" x 5 1/2" (11 cm x 14 cm)

Printing
Lithography, four Pantone colors
and metallic copper

The designer created the illustrations
with hand-cut film. The printer
ganged the cards with other jobs for
economy's sake; the set of two cards
was assembled using Macromedia
FreeHand.

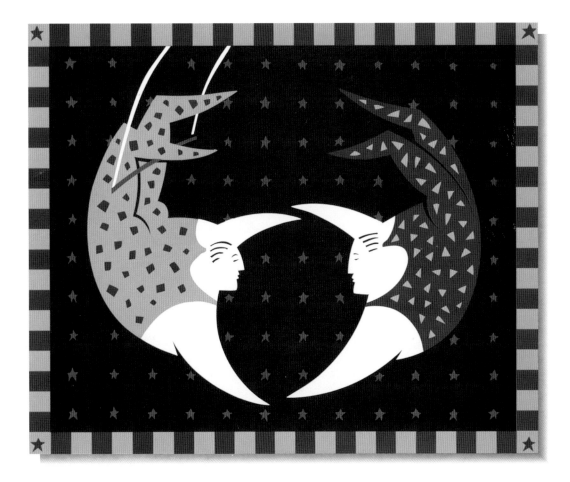

Design Firm
Misha Design Studio

Designer
Dina Barsky

Illustrator
Michael Lenn

Original Size
4" x 6" (10 cm x 15 cm)

Printing
Offset

This card promotes a one-man art show in Lowell, Massachusetts titled "Mixed Emotions." Full of brilliance and luster, the watercolor painting features a view of Lowell's city festival populated by a crowd full of mixed emotions.

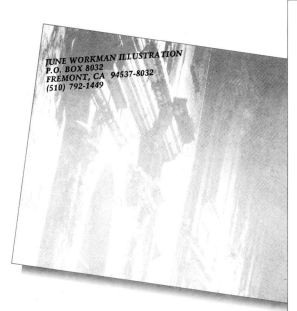

JUNE WORKMAN ILLUSTRATION
P.O. BOX 8032
FREMONT, CA 94537-8032
(510) 792-1449

JUNE WORKMAN ILLUSTRATION
(510)792-1449

Design Firm
June Workman Illustration

**Art Director/
Illustrator**
June Workman

Original Size
6" x 4" (15 cm x 10 cm)

Design Firm
T.P. Design

**Art Director/
Designer/
Illustrator**
Charly Palmer

Original Size
7" x 5" (18 cm x 13 cm)

Client
Indigo Fine Arts

Printing
4-color lithography

The artist created this piece—
titled "Blacker the Berry"—
traditionally, using acrylic and
marbleized papers. The postcard
promotes a new, open-edition
print for sale.

**Art Director/
Designer/
Illustrator**
Lynda Fishbourne

Original Size
7" x 5" (18 cm x 13 cm)

Printing
Offset

This is a series of three
postcard mailings to
promote the illustrator's
work. Painted in acrylic with
collaged pieces of paper,
the illustrations were created
for magazine articles.

Designers
Luanne D'Amico
and Grace TeSell

Original Size
4" x 6"
(10 cm x 15 cm)

Purpose/Occasion
Self-promotion

Specializing in colored pencil drawings—florals and still lifes—the artist has slides made of her work, using those to have postcards made. The designer uses these cards for invitations to shows or festivals, and for self-promotion.

Design Firm
Joan C. Hollingsworth

Art Director/Designer/Illustrator
Joan C. Hollingsworth

Photographer
Photo Art

Original Size
4" x 6" (10 cm x 15 cm)

Purpose/Occasion
Solo show promotion

Printing
Modern Postcards

The designer created this card from freehand drawings, commercial templates, handmade templates, and more than 60 years of living.

Art Director/ Photographer
Armin Vogt

Original Size
4" x 6" (10 cm x 15 cm)

Client
AVP

"Rhein" calendar—12 months,
12 cards of Rhine in each
month of the year.

Design Firm
Chase Gallery

Designer
Jeff Chase

Photographer
5,000 K, Boston

Original Size
7" x 5" (18 cm x 13 cm)

This card promoted a one-person show for Stephen Coyle at Chase Gallery. The designer created the layout in QuarkXPress.

Long Distance   48 x 44 inches   alkyd on linen

STEPHEN COYLE

AZALEA

TANIS BULA

Design Firm
TAB Graphics Design Inc.

Art Director/Designer
Tanis Bula

Photographer
Birlauf Steen

Original Size
9" x 6" (23 cm x 15 cm)

Client
TAB Gallery

The artist wanted to promote a new print, titled *Azalea;* this card does that, as well as promote her seasonal events. The large format creates a greater impact than smaller cards.

LUCIA BALDINI
Lucia Baldini
Tango — FOTOGRAFIE

Designer
Arlo Bigazzi

Original Size
4" x 6" (10 cm x 15 cm)

Client/Photographer
Lucia Baldini

Printing
Lithography

Design Firm
Mixed Nuts Inc.

Art Director/Illustrator
Bill Boyko

Designer
Cara Lynn Rumack

Original Size
6" x 4" (15 cm x 10 cm)

Purpose/Occasion
Change of address/self-promotion

Printing
4-color

Gouache, pencil, ink, and collage
with an illustrated Batman figure
keyed into the Batman movies,
popular at the time of the concept.

WHAT SHOULD YOUR DESIGN BE WINNING?

A) Awards
B) Customers

If you answered B), congratulations.
Let us award you a free consultation with a
design business that thinks like you do.
You set the agenda.
We promise to show you how good design can
win more customers for your business.
Just contact Steve Kyffin
or Mervyn Orchard...
tel or fax 01752 671783
http://www.bluestone.co.uk
If you answered A), its still not too late
to change your mind.

BLUESTONE
design consultants

Design Firm
Bluestone Design Ltd.

Art Director
S. Kyffin

Original Size
4" x 7 1/2" (10 cm x 19 cm)

Printing
Lithography

The piece, created in Adobe
Photoshop, fit into a direct-mail
push to generate awareness of the
firm before it sent the main part
of the campaign—a brochure.

Melon (Cuc...

5010©Leo1994

Design Firm
Leo Pharmaceuticals

Art Director/Designer
Vibeke Nodskov

Original Size
7 1/2" x 4" (19 cm x 10 cm)

Client
Leo Pharmaceuticals

Purpose/Occasion
Medical exhibition

Printing
4-color offset

The card, created in
QuarkXPress, is part of a
campaign for a medical
(pharmaceutical) product,
"Fucidin," and was available
at a three-day exhibition
for clients to write home.

Design Firm
Wolff Olins

Art Director/Designer
Daren Cook

Photographer
Mike Russell

Original Size
4" x 6" (10 cm x 15 cm)

Client
Citibank Credit Structures

Purpose/Occasion
Compliments/reply card

Printing
5-color lithography

These cards promote Citibank's Alpha and Beta debt investment products. To reflect that, and to emphasize the two different color identities (Alpha: green, Beta: blue), these cards were produced as an alternative to compliments slips to reinforce the product identity. No tricks were used in production; one of the ideas behind these cards is purity.

Design Firm
N.G.

Art Director/Illustrator
Makiko Azakami

Designer
Kyoko Iida

Photographer
Haruhiko Tanizaki

Original Size
4" x 10" (10 cm x 25 cm)

Printing
4-color offset printing

These hand-cut objects are formed primarily from Pantone paper, secured with double-sided adhesive tape. The designer creates these three-dimensional "paper toys" as commissioned illustrations, as well as for personal pieces. The designer created this perforated fan-postcard set as an invitation for a one-person exhibition of the designer's work at Space Yui Gallery (Tokyo) in 1994.

Johnson & Johnson

&johnson

Susan & Wayne are proud to introduce the newest
member in the Johnson family. Maegan Tayler, born on January 11, 1996,
net.wt. 8lbs. 8oz. and length 20.5 inches.

Art Director
Susan Johnson

Designer/Illustrator
Wayne M. Johnson

Original Size
3 1/2" x 5" (9 cm x 13 cm)

Client
Susan & Wayne Johnson

Purpose/Occasion
Birth announcement

Printing
2-color

Design Firm
EMA Design Inc.

Art Director
Thomas C. Ema

Designers
Thomas C. Ema,
Debra Johnson Humphrey

Original Size
10" x 6" (25 cm x 15 cm)

Client
Artist's Angle Inc.

Photographer
Stephen Ramsey

Printing
Offset

These postcards announce
and describe specific
services provided by
Artist's Angle. The designer
took the images—taken
by several photographers—
and laid them out in
Macromedia FreeHand.

GENIUS

IS THE CAPACITY TO SEE TEN THINGS

WHERE THE ORDINARY MAN SEES ONE

AND WHERE THE MAN OF TALENT SEES TWO OR THREE

E Z R A   P O U N D

A R T I S T ' S

A N G L E

I N C

Modern man learned to save time by structuring his day. The average work day is 9 am to 6 pm, minus 1 hour for lunch. That's about 10,200 days of work in an average life, without overtime. This may be a normal life in Peru, Indiana, but not in L.A. This is where design happens, along with a lot of overtime. Let us help you make that deadline on time and on budget. Our silkscreen facilities are here for you, In L.A. we may work more than those guys in Peru, but Lettergraphics just might help you get home on time to eat a hot meal.

The Aztecs loved to sacrifice entire days to ensure that the coming months would be better than the last. Great care in depicting these daily events was taken by artisans who would labor intensively for days. Overtime was given freely out of the goodness of keeping their own hearts. If only there had been a Lettergraphics silkscreen temple to go to for help. A lot of artisans would have slept peacefuly at night knowing that their job was being done for them to their specifications. We wouldn't have changed history, but we would have given them some time to play.

The Great Pyramids were the crowning glory of ancient Egypt. They were built to house the Pharaoh for his journey into the afterlife. Many years went into building these pyramids as well as the detailed tombs and murals that filled the inside. Artisans worked by candlelight for hours on end (no overtime pay existed) to show their dedication to the Pharaoh. If only the mysterious Sphinx was a Lettergraphics silkscreen shop. Our team could have helped them finish ahead of schedule and on budget. We couldn't have built the pyramids but we could have saved them some time on the decorations.

Design Firm
Evenson Design Group

Art Director
Stan Evenson

Designer
David Lomeli

Original Size
3" x 5" (8 cm x 13 cm)

Client
Lettergraphics

This postcard series promotes Lettergraphics' silkscreening services. There was a consistent theme of hard-working clients who could have benefitted from Lettergraphics' services throughout the series, which helped accurately convey the printer's point.

birthday shmirthday

Design Firm
Suburbia Studios

**Art Director/
Illustrator/
Designer**
Jeremie White

Original Size
4" x 6" (10 cm x 15 cm)

Client
Suburbia Studios

Purpose/Occasion
Birthday

Printing
Lithography, 4-color process
and metallic-tinted varnish on back

On the top half of the obverse is
a four-color scan of an oil painting;
the bottom is a close-up shot of
brushstrokes and light impasto
painting. Typeset in QuarkXPress,
printed color is metallic copper.
On the reverse is a detail of
illustration in a tinted varnish.

Design Firm
Leo Pharmaceuticals

Art Director/Designer
Vibeke Nødskov

Original Size
4" x 8" (10 cm x 20 cm)

Client
Leo Pharmaceuticals

Printing
5-color offset

The firm created this card simply because there was space left on the sheet with another project. To best use the leftover space, the designer made it as a New Year's greeting card for the staff for private use, and therefore without a company logo.

Design Firm
Cornerstone

Art Director
Keith Steimel

Designer/Illustrator
Paul McDowall,
Keith Steimel

Original Size
4" x 6" (10 cm x 15 cm)

Client
Moonlight Tobacco Co.

The object was to create a very energetic, nighttime feel for a new tobacco company. The designer used a combination of hand-drawn elements and Adobe Photoshop techniques, composing everything in Aldus FreeHand.

Design Firm
Sayles Graphic Design

Art Director
John Sayles

Designer
Jennifer Elliott

Original Size
6" x 9" (15 cm x 23 cm)

Client
Adventure Lighting

Purpose/Occasion
Promotion

Printing
Offset

Dynamic graphics and bright colors make this eye-catching postcard stand out from other mail.

Designer/Illustrator
Brian Cronin

Original Size
6" x 8" (15 cm x 20 cm)

Purpose/Occasion
Change of address

Printing
Offset

Coffee and cigarettes—a nice combination.

Design Firm
EMA Design Inc.

Art Director
Thomas C. Ema

Designers
Thomas C. Ema,
Debra Johnson Humphrey

Illustrator
Thomas C. Ema

Original Size
6" x 4" (15 cm x 10 cm)

Client
Artist's Angle Inc.

Purpose/Occasion
Various holiday greetings

Printing
Offset (Phoenix Press)

Illustrated by hand and designed on a computer, these cards were mailed in conjunction with specific holidays/seasons. They spread the word about Artist's Angle's presence in the creative community as a graphics service bureau.

Design Firm
Jean-Luc Tamisier, Paris

Designer
Jean-Luc Tamisier

Photographer
Didier Delmas, Paris

Original Size
4" x 8" (10 cm x 20 cm)

Client
Aval/Mairie de Villeneave-la-Garenne

Printing
2-color offset (black and one Pantone)

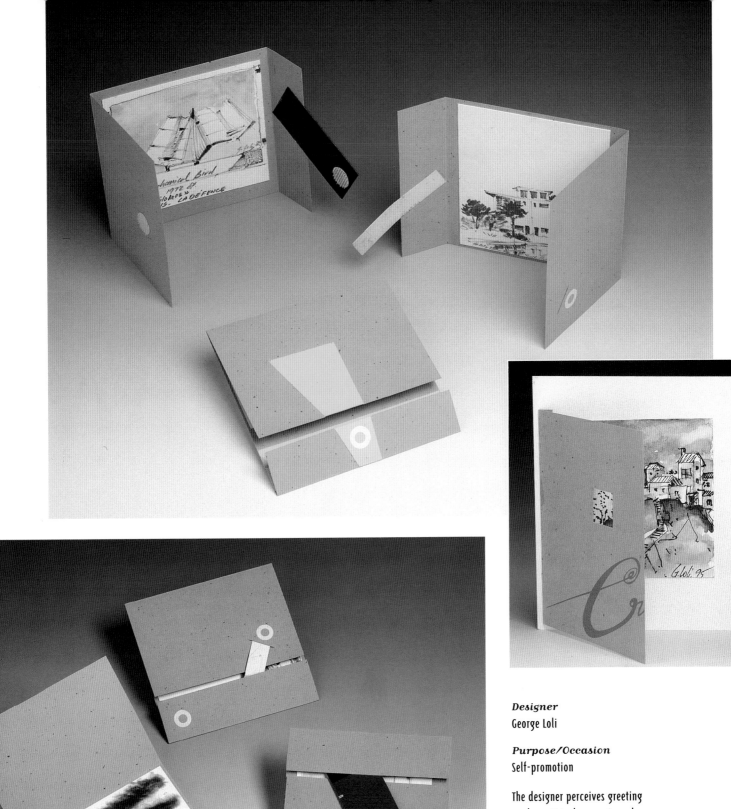

Designer
George Loli

Purpose/Occasion
Self-promotion

The designer perceives greeting cards, postcards, or notecards as very personal, an intimate extension of the sender. These cards are personal reflections, which incorporate recycled drawings, sketches, materials, and thoughts into a unique treasure.

The Chinese symbol for **crisis** has two characters. One of them 藍 means "dog". The other 柒 means "doughnut." Loosely translated, it means, "When in crisis, let out the dog, sit down and have a nice **FRESH DOUGHNUT.**"

Design Firm
Cards w/Attitude

Art Director
James Balmer

Original Size
8 1/2" x 4 1/2" (22 cm x 11 cm)

Purpose/Occasion
Miscellaneous

Printing
Laser or offset

The designer makes cards like this for fun, using a Macintosh and Adobe PageMaker. Correspondence is their main function.

Design Firm
Kan Tai-keung Design
& Associates Ltd.

Art Director
Freeman Lau Siu Hong

Designers
Freeman Lau Siu Hong,
Veronica Cheung Lai Sheung

Original Size
5" x 7" (13 cm x 18 cm)

Client
The Pottery Workshop

Created in Macromedia FreeHand, the logo for The Pottery Workshop portrays a set of pottery works. It symbolizes the various activities and functions carried out by the workshop: pottery courses, shop, exhibitions, and interest groups.

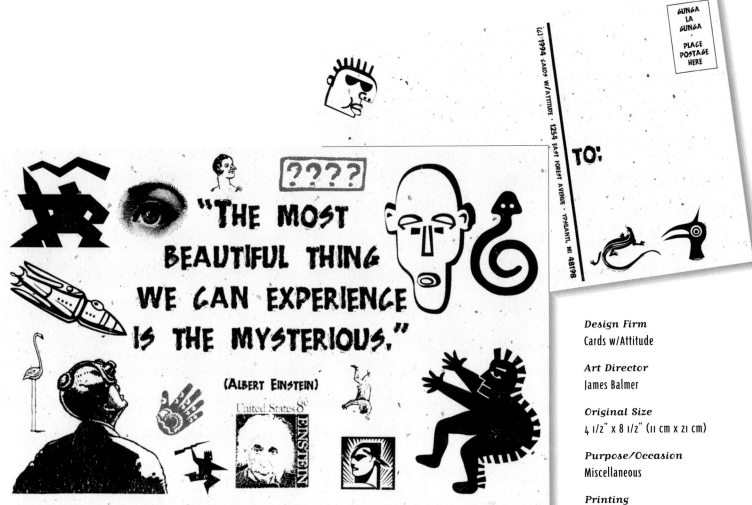

Design Firm
Cards w/Attitude

Art Director
James Balmer

Original Size
4 1/2" x 8 1/2" (11 cm x 21 cm)

Purpose/Occasion
Miscellaneous

Printing
Laser or offset

The designer makes cards like this for fun, using a Macintosh and Adobe PageMaker. Correspondence is their main function.

Design Firm
Shari Dinkins

Art Director/Designer/Illustrator/Photographer
Shari Dinkins

Original Size
4" x 6" (10 cm x 15 cm)

Printing
1-color on sheet-fed press

The designer quickly created this postcard to print with one PMS color on an uncoated, recycled-looking stock. The shaded back imagery and strange photograph caught the eye of many art directors, with promising results. The designer arranged to have the postcard gang-printed with another job to keep costs minimal.

MARSHALL WATSON

INTERIORS

New York   212   664   8094

East Hampton   516   329   1899

Design Firm
Toni Schowalter Design

Art Director/Designer
Toni Schowalter

Original Size
7" x 5" (18 cm x 13 cm)

Client
Marshall Watson Interiors

Photographer
Client supplied

Printing
4-color process/black offset

This designer used this QuarkXPress-produced card to invite clients and potential clients to a showing of Marshall Watson's work. Used later as an announcement of a magazine display, this card is still used by Watson to inform clients of future events.

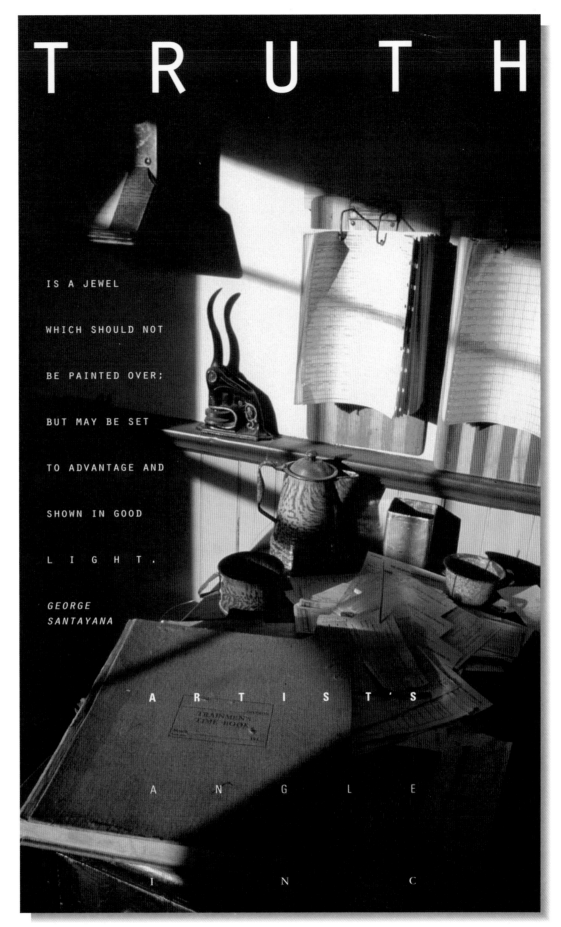

Design Firm
EMA Design Inc.

Art Director
Thomas C. Ema

Designer
Thomas C. Ema,
Debra Johnson Humphrey

Photographer
Michael Lewis

Original Size
10" x 6" (25 cm x 15 cm)

Client
Artist's Angle Inc.

Printing
Offset

These postcards announce and
describe specific services provided
by Artist's Angle. The designer took
the images—taken by several
photographers—and laid them out
in Macromedia FreeHand.

Design Firm
Free-Range Chicken Ranch

Art Director
Tony Parmley

Designer
Kelli Christman

Illustrator
Donna Gilbert

Original Size
4" x 6" (10 cm x 15 cm)

Client
The Flying Logo Sisters

Printing
Offset

A unique company with a unique name wanted something bright and fun to announce their move—the card features fluorescent ink and black on fluorescent stock. The designer laid out the hand-made illustrations and type in QuarkXPress.

Advertising Firm
Bremble & Sewforth

Art Director/Designer
Leslie Mullen

Illustrator
Charlie Hill, Super Stock

Original Size
3 1/2" x 5 1/2" (9 cm x 14 cm)

Client
American Chemical Society Publications

Purpose/Occasion
Ad sales promotion

Printing
Heidelberg press

With permission from Super Stock photo agency, the original image, "Decision Makers" by Charlie Hill, was manipulated on the Mac in Adobe Photoshop to enlarge the computer monitor, change the proportion of the people, move a woman into the group and "flip" the total image. Also, the designer created a grayscale version for the reverse.

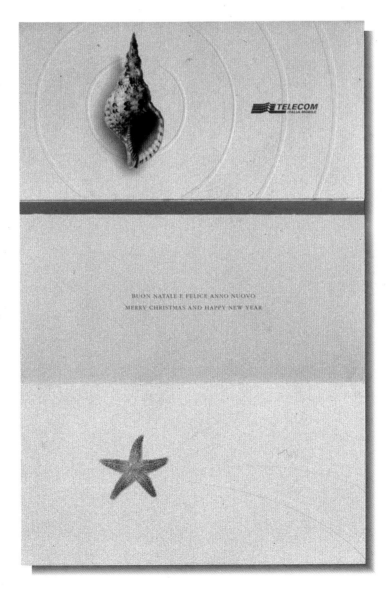

Design Firm
Sheehan Design

Art Director/Designer
Jamie Sheehan

Illustrator
Jamie Sheehan/Art Chantry

Original Size
4" x 9" (10 cm x 23 cm)

Client
Jobe Waterskis

Printing
Silk screen on aluminum

The purpose of the postcard was to let retailers view a wakeboard (and how it worked) prior to placing orders. Since the board was designed to be three-dimensional, it was necessary to show how it worked. The firm printed the cards using misprints of aluminum wakeboard covers, making them cost-effective and sensible.

Design Firm
Area-Strategic Design

Art Director/Designer
Stefano Avrey

Photographer
Giuseppe Fadda

Original Size
4 1/2" x 8 1/2" (11 cm x 21 cm)

Client
Telecon Italia Mobile

Purpose/Occasion
Christmas greeting

Printing
Lithography

The embossing shows the message—radio waves—over everything; the shell for Christmas becomes a shooting star.

Art Director
Holly Maiter

Designer
Susan Utterback

Original Size
4" x 6" (10 cm x 15 cm)

Client
South Suburban College

Purpose/Occasion
Announcement

Printing
Black plus (1) PMS color

The designer composed this postcard in Adobe PageMaker, manipulating the type and graphic on the obverse in Illustrator.

Designer
Arlo Bigazzi

Photographer
Lucia Baldini

Original Size
6" x 4" (15 cm x 10 cm)

Client
Hateriali Sonori

Purpose/Occasion
CD release

Printing
Lithography

Design Firm
Carole Goodman

**Art Director/Designer/
Illustrator/Photographer**
Carole Goodman

Original Size
6" x 9" (15 cm x 23 cm)

Printing
Silk screen

This is a study/sketch made for a movie. The artworks convey two different experiences occurring during two different eras, in the same place.

Design Firm
Télé Québec

Art Director
Jean Segers

Photographer
J. P. Danwye

Original Size
3 1/2" x 8" (9 cm x 20 cm)

Client
Télé Québec

This was a giveaway for kids at fairs, in hopes they would stick them all over.

Do the math! Buy two units of Sidekick 95. the #1 best-selling personal organizer, and get an NFR Dashboard 95 free! (or vice-versa) They're both 100% Windows 95 compliant and 100% 32-bit native. But hurry. this is a limited time offer! Call your distributor now!

INGRAM MICRO

1-800-456-8000

Limit one per reseller location.

1600 E. St. Andrew Place
P.O. Box 25125
Santa Ana, CA 92799-5125

Starfish Software™

now shipping!

Just buy two

Starfish

Software

Windows® 95

applications,

and get one

free. Get it?

one, two, free!

(what are you waiting for??!!)

Design Firm
Free-Range Chicken Ranch

Art Director/Designer
Kelli Christman

Original Size
4" x 6" (10 cm x 15 cm)

Photographer
Jeff Becker

Printing
Offset

The firm needed something bright and eye-catching to introduce new product versions. The man screaming in the background helps emphasize the headline; the recycled photo retains its moiré pattern to add interest.

Buy two units of Sidekick 95. the #1 best-selling personal organizer. and get an NFR Dashboard 95 free! (or vice-versa) They're both 100% Windows 95 compliant and 100% 32-bit native. You've only got until 11/20/95. so order now!

Tech Data
CORPORATION

1-800-237-8931

Limit one per reseller location.

5350 Tech Data Drive
Clearwater, FL 34620

now shipping!

Starfish Software™

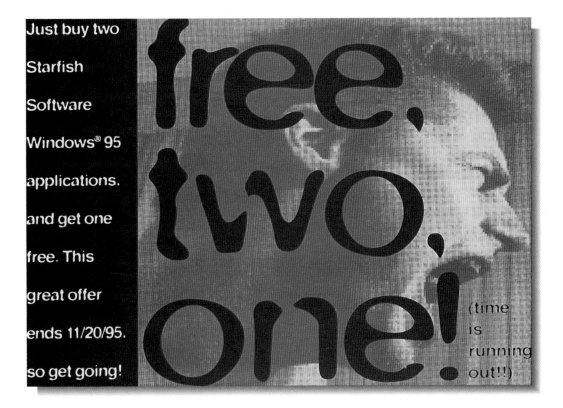

Just buy two Starfish Software Windows® 95 applications. and get one free. This great offer ends 11/20/95. so get going!

free, two, one! (time is running out!!)

Design Firm
My Table

Art Director
Byrne-Dodge

Original Size
5" x 3 1/2" (13 cm x 9 cm)

Illustrator
Brian Kirchner

Printing
Offset

This was the designer's first foray into color—*My Table*, a bimonthly dining-out magazine, is black-and-white only— and she wanted a promotional/ direct-response piece that would reflect the whimsical, un-slick quality of the publication. The card brought a 10 percent response; even better were the compliments from the many people who liked the card.

Love to Eat Out?

YOU ARE INVITED TO TRY A TASTE OF

my table

FREE!

THE ONLY PUBLICATION DEDICATED SOLELY TO DINING OUT IN HOUSTON.

★

my table
A Critic's Guide to Dining in Houston

YOU CAN ENJOY A **FREE** SAMPLE ISSUE AND RECEIVE A VERY SPECIAL SUBSCRIPTION OFFER BY FILLING OUT AND RETURNING THIS EXCLUSIVE *RSVP* INVITATION! Discover for yourself why John Mariani, restaurant critic for *Esquire* magazine, calls Teresa Byrne-Dodge's journal "both indispensable and a joy to read."

Please fill out and mail this *RSVP* card to receive your **FREE** sample issue of *my table* and a special subscription offer.

NAME_____
ADDRESS_____
CITY _____
STATE _____ ZIP _____

my table
9337-B KATY FREEWAY, #271
HOUSTON, TX 77024

Design Firm
Segura Inc.

Art Director
Carlos Segura

Designer
Jon Stepping,
Carlos Segura

Original Size
6" x 9" (15 cm x 23 cm)

Client
Q101 Radio

Purpose/Occasion
Promotion

Printing
4-color

Postcard series targeted
to media buyers for
Q101 Radio.

Design Firm
84 Lumber

Designer
Rene Klodowski

Original Size
5" x 7" (13 cm x 18 cm)

Printing
Four Pantone colors

The designer created this
direct response piece—
encouraging contractors to
attend a builder's show—
in QuarkXPress, using
artwork created in
Adobe Illustrator with
four spot colors.

Art Director
Ida Cheinman

Designers
Ida Cheinman, Rick Salzman

Original Size
5 1/2" x 12" (14 cm x 31 cm)

Client
Interactive Entertainment Magazine

Printing
4-color offset

The designer created this piece with Macromedia FreeHand, Adobe Photoshop, and QuarkXPress. The designer intended to give the cards a contemporary look, reiterating the ambience and energy of *Interactive Entertainment Magazine*, a CD-ROM computer gaming publication. The piece provides two business reply mail cards and a bonus postcard.

Design Firm
Dean Johnson Design

Art Director
Bruce Dean

Designer
Patricia Prather

Copywriter
Rob Holder

Photographer
Wilbur Montgomery,
WM Photographic Services

Original Size
7" x 5" (18 cm x 13 cm)

Client
Walker Group

This clever campaign solicited new business
in consumer/product research arena.
The concept was to show that objects near
and dear—recognizable American icons—may
not have been so easy to market and sell.

The patio at Pane e Vino Los Angeles

Design Firm
Dyer/Mutchnick Group Inc.

Designer
Rod Dyer

Illustrator
Harriet Baba

Original Size
5" x 7" (13 cm x 18 cm)

Client
Pane e Vino Restaurant

INDEX

DIRECTORY

DIRECTORY

Ads To Go Inc. 5821 Cedar Lake Road, Minneapolis, MN 55416

After Hours Creative 1201 E. Jefferson B100, Phoenix, AZ 85034

Area-Strategic Design V. Legorizia 52 00981, Rome, Italy

Art Chantry P.O. Box 4069, Seattle, WA 98104

Artbank Editions 21 Elms Road, London SW4 9ER. UK

Athanasius Design 1300 North Damen Avenue, Chicago, IL 60622

Bartels & Company 3284 Ivanhoe Road, St. Louis, MO 63139

Becker Design 225 E. St. Paul Avenue, Suite 300, Milwaukee, WI 53202

Beckman Instruments 2500 N. Harbor Blvd. #B-23, Fullerton, CA 92635-2600

Belyea Design Alliance 1809 Seventh Avenue, Suite 1007, Seattle, WA 98101

Bethanie Deeney 31 E. 31st Street #12C, New York, NY 10016

Big Road Blue 66A Elm Park Road, London N3 1EB England

Arlo Bigazzi V. 3 Novembre, 2, 52027 S. Giovanni, Italy

Bill Nelson Illustration Inc. 107 East Cary Street, Richmond, VA 23219

Bluestone Design Ltd. 87 Mannamead Road, Plymouth Devon UK

Kevin Bond 1930 Sacramento Street, San Francisco, CA 94109-3423

Bremble & Sewforth 3530 Rt. 27, Kendall Park, NJ 08824

Brian Shore, Architect 90 Forest Avenue, Locust Valley, NY 11560-1714

Britches of Georgetowne 544 Herdon Parkway, Herdon, VA 22070

C. Carp Designs P.O. Box 1689, Laytonville, CA 95454

Cards w/Attitude 2598 Esch Avenue, Ann Arbor, MI 48104

Carole Goodman 50 Lexington Avenue, Number 4E, New York, NY 48303

Charles Carpenter Illustration and Design 2724 South Armacost West, Los Angeles, CA 90064

Chase Gallery 173 Newbury Street, Boston, MA 02116

Ida Cheinman and Rick Salzman P.O. Box 1825, Plattsburgh NY 12901-0260

Chermayeff & Geismar Inc. 15 East 26th Street, New York, NY 10010

Joe Ciardiello 2182 Clove Road, Staten Island, NY 10305

Cindy Wrobel, Design & Illustration 415 Alta Dena, St. Louis, MO 63145

Clownbank Studio P.O. Box 7709, 2573 Misson Street, Santa Cruz, CA 95060

Jaqueline Comstock 17 Oakland Court, Warwick, NY 10990

Cook and Shanosky Assoc. Inc. 401 S. State Street, Newtown, PA 18940

Cornerstone 444 Park Avenue S., New York, NY 10016

Cosaro and Associates 640 Sunset Drive, Naperville, IL 60540

Brian Cronin 682 Broadway, New York, NY 10012

Luanne D'Amico and Grace TeSelle Rt. 2 Box 42, Alachua, FL 32615

David Bamundo Illustration 146 Chandler Avenue, Staten Island, NY 10314

Dean Johnson Design 604 Ft. Wayne Avenue, Indianapolis, IN 46204

Sharon DeLaCruz P.O. Box 11715, Chicago, IL 60611

Design Center 15119 Minnetonka, Minnetonka, MN 95345

The Design Company 79 Kirkland Street, Cambridge MA 02138-2071

Design Factory 59 Merrion Square, Dublin 2 Ireland

Design Ranch 335 S. Clinton, Iowa City, IA 52240

Design Studio Selby 600 S.E. Powell Boulevard, Portland, Oregon 97202

Diane Woods 919 Sheridan Avenue, Cody, WY 82414

Dragon's Teeth Design 419 College Avenue, Greensburg, PA 15601

Duo Design 250 W. 99th St. #9C, New York, NY 10025

Dyer/Mutchnick Group Inc. 8360 Melrose Avenue, 3rd Floor,
    Los Angeles, CA 90069

Dynamo c/o 50 Percy Lane, Ballsbridge, Dublin 4, Ireland

84 Lumber Rt. 519 Box 8484, Eighty Four, PA 15384

Elmwood Elmwood House, Ghyll Royd, Guiseley, Leeds, GB

EMA Design Inc. 1128 15th Street #301, Denver, CO 80204

Evenson Design Group 4445 Overland Avenue, Colver City, CA 90230

Lynda Fishbourne 195 Hemenway Road, Framingham, MA 01701

Fordesign P.O. Box 13662. Alexandria, LA 71315

Franek Design Associates Inc. 5101 Wisconsin Avenue NW,
    Washington DC 20016-4120

Free-Range Chicken Ranch 330A East Campbell Street, Campbell, CA 95008

Fresno Pacific College 1717 S. Chestnut Avenue, Fresno, CA 93702-4709

Maria Friske 180 St. Paul St. # 201-B, Rochester, NY 14604

Future Studio P.O. Box 292000, Los Angeles, CA 90029

Gackel Anderson Henningsen Inc. 2415 18th Street, Suite 107,
    Bettendorf, IA 52722

George Samerjan 201 Apple Tree Lane, Brewster, NY 10509

Rebecca Grimes 936 Stone Road, Westminster, MD 21158

Heather Yale Creative 153 Federal Street, Salem, MA 01970

Hilton International, Bankok At Nai Lert Park., 2 Wireless Road, Bankok

Honblue Inc. 501 Sumner Street 3B1, Honolulu, HI 96816-4213

Howard Levy Design 40 Cindy Lane, Ocean, NJ 07712

Insight Design Communications 700 S. Marcilene, Wichita, KS 67218

Dennis Irwin 412 Leland Avenue, Palo Alto, CA 94306

Jean-Luc Tamisier 2 bis, rue de Nice, 75011 Paris

Joan C. Hollingsworth 2824 NE 22 Avenue, Portland, OR 97212

Wayne M. Johnson 2347 Materhorn Road, Dallas, TX 75228

June Workman Illustration 419 Mason Street, Suite 200,
    Vacaville, CA 95688

Kan Tai-keung Design & Associates Ltd. 28/F Great Smart Tower,
    230 Wanchai Road, Hong Kong

Ken Weightman Design 7036 Park Drive, New Port Richey, FL 34652

Eric Kohler 280 Riverside Drive #141, New York, NY 10025

Gary Krueger P.O. Box 543, Montrose, CA 91021

Lamont-Doherty Earth Observatory P.O. Box 1000 1Rt. 9W,
    Palisades, NY 10964

Leo Pharmaceuticals Industriparken 55, DK-2750 Ballerup

The Leonhardt Group 1218 3rd Avenue #620, Seattle, WA 98101

Lev Laboratorio di Comunicazione 3 Ebony House, Lithos Road,
    NW3 6EA London

George Loli 116 St. Julien Way, Lafayette, LA 70506

Lorraine Williams Illustration 36 Plaza St. E. #43, Brooklyn, NY 11238

Marcolina Design Inc. 1100 E. Hector Street, Suite 400,
    Conshohocken, PA 19428

Mário Aurélio & Associates Rua Cidade do Recife 232 3E, 4200 Porto

Mars 24209 Southwestern, Southfield, MI 48075

Maverick Art Tribe 112 C 17th Avenue NW, Calgary AB CAn T2M 0M6

Hal Mayforth 108 E. 35 Street, New York, NY 10016

Mervil Paylor Design 1917 Lennox Avenue, Charlotte, NC 28203

Midget Design 53 Torey Cresent, Victoria, BC V9o 1A4, Canada

MGM Illustration 401 NW 1 Avenue, Ft. Lauderdale, FL 33301

Mike Salisbury Communications Inc. 2200 Amapola Ct., Suite 202, Torrance, CA 90501

Misha Design Studio 1638 Commonwealth Avenue Ste. 24, Boston, MA 02135

Mixed Nuts Inc. 16 Conrad Avenue, Toronto, Canada M6G 3G5

Mustardseed Enterprises P.O. Box 932, No. Chatham, NY 12132

My Table 9337-B Katy Freeway #271, Houston, TX 77024

N.G. 4-1-8 Hiro Shibu Ya-Ku, Tokyo

Paper Shrine 604 France Street, Baton Rouge LA 70802

Paul Stoddard Illustration 524 Main Street, Stoneham, MA 02180

Kari Payment 1815 Manor Haven, Ortonville, MI 48462

Richard Puder Design 2 West Blackwell Street, Dover, NJ 07802

Rosenworld 45 Lispenard Street, New York, NY 10013

Sagmeister Inc. 222 West 14th Street, New York, NY 10016

Ann Samul 11 Pacific Street, New London, CT 06320

Sayles Graphic Design 308 Eighth Street, New York, NY 10016

Schudlich Design Illustration 1064 Milwaukee, Denver, CO 80206

Segura Inc. 361 W. Chestnut Street, Chicago, IL 60612

Shamlian Advertising 128 Mansion Drive, Media, PA 19063

Shari Dinkins P.O. Box 1354, Pacifica, CA 94044

Sheehan Design 500 Aurora Avenue N., Suite #404, Seattle, WA 98109

So Yoon Lym 621 Farmdale Road, Franklin Lakes, NJ 07417-1151

Standard Deluxe Inc. Doolittle Lane, Waverly, AL 36879

James Steinberg 108 E. 35 St., New York, NY 10016

Studio Guarnaccia 31 Fairfield Street, Montclair, NJ 07042

Suburbia Studios 53 Tovey Crescent, Victoria, BC V9o 1A4, Canada

Superstock Inc. 7660 Centurion Parkway, Jacksonville, FL 32256

TAB Graphics Design Inc. 1120 Lincoln Street, Suite 700, Denver, CO 80203

Télé Québec 1000 Fulleum Street, Montreal, Quebec H2K 3L7

Thompson Design Group 524 Union Street, San Francisco, CA 94133

Thompson/Kerr 8384 Lakeshore Circle #3326, Indianapolis, IN 46250

Tieken Design & Creative Services 2800 N. Central Avenue #150, Phoenix, AZ 85004

Tim Ernst Cartoons Maison Ishikawa B302, 16-26 Yabase Shinkawamukai Akita-Shi, Akita-Ken, Japan 010

T.P. Design 7007 Eagle Watch Court, Stone Mountain, GA 30087

Toni Schowalter Design 1133 Broadway, New York, NY 10010

Troller Assoc. 12 Harbor Lane, Rye, NY 10580

Susan Utterback South Suburban College, 15800 S. State Street, South Holland, IL 60473

Visible Ink 678 13th Street #202, Oakland, CA 94612

Armin Vogt Munsterplatz 8, CH-4001 Basel

Walker Pinfold Associates (London Ltd.) 17, The Ivories, 6 Northampton St London N1 2HY England

Frank Wiedemann 2077 Fulton Street, San Francisco, CA 94117

Wolff Olins 10 Regents Wharf, All Saints Street, London, N1 9RL

XJR Design 700 N. Green Street, Chicago, IL 60622

Ulana Zahajkewycz 26 The Crescent, Montclair, NJ 07042